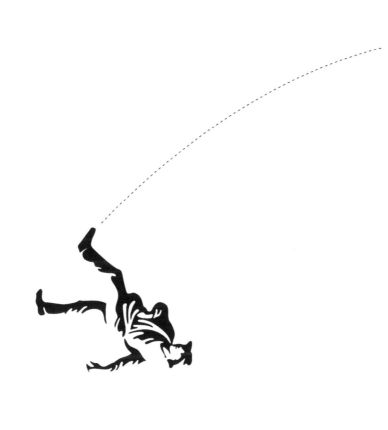

HARVEY ARATON

Alive and Kicking

When Soccer Moms Take the Field and Change Their Lives Forever

Simon & Schuster

New York   London   Toronto   Sydney   Singapore

SIMON & SCHUSTER
Rockefeller Center
1230 Avenue of the Americas
New York, NY 10020

SIMON & SCHUSTER and colophon are registered trademarks
of Simon & Schuster, Inc.

For information regarding special discounts for bulk purchases,
please contact Simon & Schuster Special Sales at 1-800-456-6798
or business@simonandschuster.com

Book design by Ellen R. Sasahara

Manufactured in the United Sates of America

1 3 5 7 9 10 8 6 4 2

Library of Congress Cataloging-in-Publication Data
Araton, Harvey.
Alive and kicking : when soccer moms take the field and change their lives
forever / Harvey Araton.
p. cm.
1. Soccer for women—New Jersey. I. Title
GV944.5 .A73 2001
796.334'082—dc21   2001031307
ISBN 13: 978-1-4165-7517-7   ISBN 10: 1-4165-7517-0

To the memory of Milly Klingman,
who redirected her life in midstream
to rescue so many others

Contents

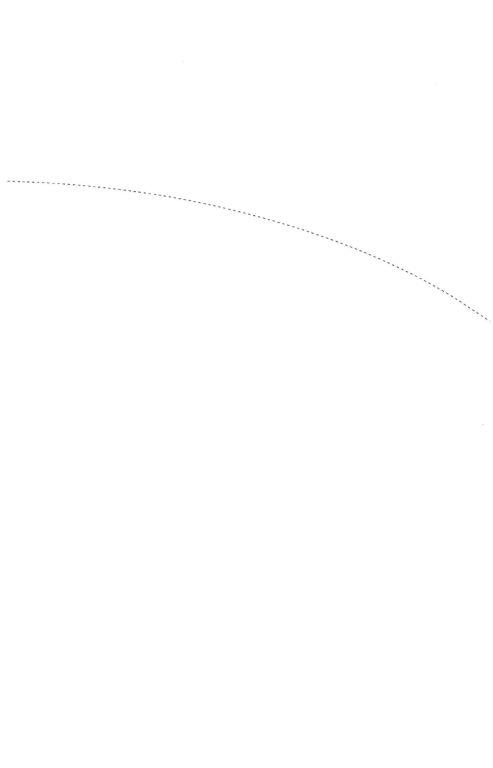

Introduction

T HE FIRST SPORTS TEAMS I can recall being a member of were impromptu groupings in the school yard outside Public School 165, in the Brownsville section of Brooklyn, during the early 1960s. My family lived in the brick-faced apartment building right across the street, on Hopkinson Avenue. When my mother inevitably poked her head out the fourth-floor window to summon me for dinner, the game was over, until the next day.

I wasn't the best punchball player in the neighborhood, not by the proverbial long shot. I wasn't the home-run threat, the one blessed with the most potent fist. I did have a knack for hitting the part of the school that jutted into the school yard in what was right-center field; we called it the Short Wall. A Spaldeen lofted just right would strike the wall's upper half—without landing and getting lost on the roof—and was an almost automatic double. I had the knack, and, invariably, one of the self-appointed team captains would, after suspiciously eyeing the lot of us, blurt out: "We got Harvey." It was done: I was chosen in, conditioned to the thrill of peer inclusion at the tender age of eight.

My wife had to wait until she was forty. She experienced that particular high for the first time during the winter of 1999, several months after she had whimsically begun playing soccer with a group of other mothers in our town, Montclair, New Jersey. The women had been invited to play in a new league by the organizers of a brand-new indoor facility. They were forming teams, and there was some anxiety about how the sides were going to be formed.

Beth got off the phone one night, her face atypically flush.

"What's the matter?" I asked.

"Lisa and Ginger want me to be on their team," she said, referring to two of the better players. Her face was reddening, and out of the corner of her eye escaped a tear. "No one's ever asked me to be on a team before," she said, this childlike confession from a public relations executive and mother of two.

When it comes to recreational sports, I consider my wife the more diverse athlete. She grew up in Greenwich, Connecticut, an affluent suburb, while I was raised in more modest, urban New York City settings. For much of her life she could sail and ski and skate, while I somehow emerged from years of summer camp without so much as learning to stay afloat in water over my head. I did play team sports, though: Back in that Brownsville school yard, we played the street games of the day—punchball, stickball, and long-abandoned contrivances like off-the-wall. On those enduring afternoons I learned how to be a teammate, a moderator, a friend, sometimes a hero, occasionally the goat. None of that mattered as much as the opportunity to play, to belong. The most rewarding constant was the camaraderie, the sharing. Right through high school and into my early adult life, I took this treat for granted, the entitlement of being an athletic boy.

Introduction

My wife, Beth Albert, was, as a child, a musician, a flutist and pianist. Now, while I have taken up piano in my forties and relish the opportunity to play solo, she returns from her soccer games and scrimmages with a radiance, a new sense of self found in her immersion in her team. I can see it in her body language, her newly choreographed strut, evident even as she pulls off a dirty, sweaty sock.

She regales our two boys, both youth players, with elaborate soccer tales. They show off their newest ball tricks to each other out on the front lawn. She bounces out of bed on Sundays, stating her domestic priorities by putting on her cleats and rushing off to practice. We go at night as a family to watch her play, to root her on. She tells me that she dreams about the game, about making exotic moves. Her friends call and talk endlessly about upcoming games, about players they like or fear on other teams. They are a close-knit group, speaking a language only they understand. And it is not without envy that I recall these uplifting feelings I have not had in years, feelings she is experiencing for the first time.

"I wish I'd had this my whole life," she said wistfully the night her team won its first big game, a showdown between two unbeaten teams.

In my work as a sports columnist for *The New York Times,* it has become more difficult with each passing year to find people who feel as good about sports as Beth does now. I too often chronicle the misadventures of millionaire athletes who play for billionaire owners, who, together with the corporate underwriters and network monoliths, have perpetuated a profit- and greed-driven system that drains the joy and civility from our games.

Seldom, it seems, is sport what we long romanticized it to be, or what we still abstractly believe it should be. We've had to desensitize ourselves to the guilt and disgust we feel about the kinds of people on whom we're spending staggering sums to go see play. Only in increasingly rare moments are the games—even those of the Olympic variety—about the purity of competition anymore. You have to look harder now, and often in places we wouldn't have looked before, to find those who play for reasons other than celebrity and wealth.

The most extraordinary athlete I've met during two decades of covering sports, in fact, had neither. Diana Golden Brosnihan had her cancer-ridden right leg amputated at the age of twelve, and she proceeded to become a disabled Olympic and world-champion skier. When she was an adult, her life became more calamitous, as she lost both breasts and the ability to bear children. She was undergoing grueling chemotherapy yet again when I met and interviewed her in New York several years ago, on the day she was being honored by the Women's Sports Foundation. I will never forget the way her husband, Steve, gently massaged her back on their hotel room bed as he listened to his frail yet beautiful thirty-four-year-old wife tell of how she had attempted suicide—and celebrated her failure by climbing Mount Rainier. Steve Brosnihan had played baseball at Dartmouth, where he remembered watching Diana running the stadium steps, on crutches. He intuitively knew this was a person he wanted to meet. "Compared to Diana," he admitted, "I can't even consider myself an athlete."

Before her latest go-round with cancer, Diana had made more than her share of motivational speeches on various lecture circuits. It had been not so much for money, less so for status, and certainly not for sympathy; it was more, she said, for recognition on two most formidable fronts. "Women's sports were once in the same place as disabled sports," she said. "People would see you play and say, 'How sweet,' and you wanted to scream, 'This is about passion, about fire, about being an athlete.'"

Just about the time soccer was taking root in Beth's life, I went off to cover the 1999 women's college basketball Final Four in San Jose, California. In the championship game, Purdue's two senior stars, Stephanie White-McCarty and Ukari Figgs, squared off against Duke and two former teammates who had left Purdue three years before to protest a coaching change. A bitterly contested game went down to the last four minutes, then, suddenly, White-McCarty sprained her ankle and limped off in tears. "I have to go back, I have to," she cried, while being held by teammates on the sideline. Finally, Figgs, a black woman from Kentucky, hugged White-McCarty, a white woman from Indiana.

"I love you," Figgs told her. "I'm going to win it for you." And that's what she did.

Watching the game on television and then reading my column about that sideline drama the following morning, Beth later told me she had a new appreciation for the players' relationship, for what they experienced together. It reminded her of a soccer game she had recently played in, when her teammate Clare Moore took an early shot to the chest, could barely breathe, and spent the rest of the game on the sideline, doubled over.

"You feel this closeness and common cause of self-preservation you can't even describe," Beth said. "It's almost like love."

In most cases, the Montclair soccer moms are women whose daughters have been the beneficiaries of Title IX, the 1972 federal legislation that guaranteed equal athletic access for girls. In 1970 only one in twenty-seven girls participated in high school sports. Today it's one in three. There are almost 2.5 million American girls participating on a high school sports team and many more millions of younger girls involved in grassroots programs. But as I looked around the country, I noticed that their mothers—women who for much of their lives had little or no access to America's playing fields—were also crossing the sidelines in surprisingly large numbers.

Women raised in communities that didn't give girls' athletics a passing thought have had to overcome disabilities beyond undeveloped skills. In many cases they had no frame of reference, no understanding of how to be a team-sport athlete. They suddenly found themselves in the new and vulnerable position of being accountable, of being at risk of failing their friends. But I met so many women who say that they've long wanted at least to try.

"In one generation, we've gone from hoping there was a team to hoping to make the team," said Professor Mary Jo Kane, director of the Tucker Center for Research on Girls and Women in Sport at the University of Minnesota, when I called to ask about studies on "older" women's sports. "Watching their own daughters get the opportunities they never had has impacted on the pre–Title IX women. It's made them fight back against the idea that team sports were subversive in terms of femininity. But this is something that has largely been ignored by scholars and the press."

Largely, but not completely: A few weeks after Beth and her friends began kicking the ball around in the park on Wednesday mornings, I wrote an article in the Sunday New Jersey supplement of *The New York Times,* under the headline SOCCER PLAYING MOMS. Suddenly, wherever I went in town, people would regale me with stories of a woman they knew—a relative, a friend, or the friend of a friend—who had taken up a sport with unequivocal adult passion.

On the Lifecycle at the Y, I was told of a woman who was swimming and playing water polo in Manhattan. I called her, and Lisa Springer, forty-two, said she believed that the discipline of sports had helped her complete her first novel. She said that when she swam a five-mile race with a friend across Chesapeake Bay to celebrate turning forty, her mother and sister went to the medical tent instead of the finish line to look for her. "They expected me to fail, which was the usual perception in my family," she said. She didn't fail, and perhaps she changed those perceptions forever.

Picking up my children at school, I spoke to a woman who had recently moved out from Brooklyn and whose friend was playing hockey. When I called her, Cristina Delgado, a forty-year-old director of development at the Brooklyn Museum of Art, told me she had taken up the sport simultaneously with her young son, August. She invited me to a game on a weekday winter night, and we decided to meet at her apartment in Brooklyn Heights. She was late arriving from work, having been summoned by her boss just as she was about to leave. "I was sitting there, looking at the clock go round and thinking that if he doesn't stop talking soon, I may have to scream, 'I've got a hockey game tonight!'"

We drove toward the Riverbank Arena, out on the Hudson River in Washington Heights. In a typical Manhattan traffic snarl, Cristina recalled how she and her son had gone together to purchase their first hockey equipment, how August had been bursting with excitement, rushing into the bedroom to change when they got home. Cristina had to help, of course, attaching the bulky pads to his skinny legs and lacing up the skates and strapping the helmet on.

"How do I look?" August said.

"Like Wayne Gretzky," his mother said.

Then it was her turn, and she, too, couldn't wait. Cristina had always loved sports, especially team sports, growing up as the youngest of four sisters born in Havana. She'd played basketball and field hockey in high school, in Hamden, Connecticut, and even some club basketball at Oberlin College. Then the games were out of her life, presumably forever, until she heard that the Brooklyn Blades youth hockey program also had a program for women. She met a woman ten years her senior named Kathy Berlinger, a family therapist who told her that hockey had reinvigorated her life to the point where she often cited it to female clients who came to her to help save their foundering marriages.

With August already decked out in that equipment on shopping day, Cristina gathered her own gear, retreated into the bedroom, and slipped into it as fast as she could. Helmet on, stick in hand, she waddled out of the bedroom onto the rug.

"How does Mommy look?" she asked, her arms spread wide.

August just stared at her, hard. "That looks stupid," he said, dropping his stick and stomping off to his room.

Cristina stood there, frozen on her blades, her Kodak moment effectively quashed. "And I knew right then," she told me, "that to raise this boy to respect women in the way I wanted him to, I just had to play."

The more I looked, the more I discovered that Professor Kane was absolutely right: There was a story developing, largely untouched and untold, of mature, adult women finding any available time and place to get up a game. They were rowing down the Charles River in Boston, shooting baskets in Virginia, whipping footballs around Central Park.

This was in the winter and spring of 1999, months before the U.S. World Cup women's soccer team would become, in a year of banner sports news, the biggest story of all, the *Sports Illustrated* Sportswomen of the Year. In a season of endless nominations of best ever, women occupied the cover at millennium's end.

Even before Mia and Brandi and Kristine were filling stadiums and scoring groundbreaking television ratings, my wife and her friends had an overwhelming sense that something was happening, and it wasn't too late, and they wanted in. Maybe hockey was a bit much, given the equipment required and the ice-time constraints. Maybe their gravitating to the sport their children were playing was logical and inevitable. If it is true that the more we age, the closer we are to being childlike again, then why not soccer? Two shin guards. A pair of cleats. A ball. A field, marked by a few orange cones. It couldn't be coincidence that they were choosing a sport that, no matter how big it grew, maintained its human dimensions.

What amazed me most about my wife and her friends was how quickly their years of denial vanished when they hit that field. Sport mattered to them. The game mattered. It soon become clear that there was going to be no turning back—not for most of them, or for the people in their lives.

One night Beth was leaving the house for a game as the Knicks were about to play their archrival Miami in the NBA play-offs. I gave our sons the choice of going to watch Mom play or staying home with Dad to watch the big basketball game. They marched out with Beth, promising to behave. As the door closed and I settled back on the couch with the clicker and the chips, I felt a touch of exhilaration, a sense of triumph for their choice.

The Knicks were, as usual, a huge springtime sports story in the New York area. They were a classic dysfunctional team, and their disharmonic tales were filling the columns of the sports sections daily. Their star, Latrell Sprewell, was best known for choking a coach. The Knicks were owned by Cablevision, the cold, expansive sports-and-cable-television corporate empire. Having covered pro basketball in the city for many years, I had several close friends who were shelling out hundreds of dollars for a single ticket, and admitting they often questioned their own sanity for doing so.

Each night as they walked into Madison Square Garden, they rationalized, it was with the hope that the Knicks would reward them with a display of collective passion. The fans loved the game, what it represented, what it could be. But when you stripped away all the years of conditioning and hype, you realized that, for little or no cost, and with no sense of shame, you could find places where players delivered affection and effort, every single time they laced up.

One morning at about the same time, in a restaurant on Manhattan's Upper West Side, I was interviewing Billie Jean King, who belongs on every list of the most original, authentic, and respected athletes of the twentieth century. She recalled a childhood incident when she was made to feel unwelcome because she was the only girl among all the boys at a tennis club clinic. Someone came to her defense that day, and she has wondered through the years if that was a crossroads for her: Might her life have been radically different if one or two seemingly small events had never occurred?

"It's possible I might never had played sports at all," she said.

I casually mentioned Beth and her soccer-playing friends—how they had, after years of being denied, stood up for themselves, for the right to play. Her eyes widened. I could detect a tiny smile of satisfaction curling at the corner of her mouth. This, after all, was part of her legacy at work.

"The courage of these women, just to try after being denied so long, is amazing," she said. "Just getting out there, saying the hell with cellulite, is a victory in itself." She paused, sipping from her cup. "You know what?" she said. "I would want to know their stories, each and every one."

Right at that moment I wanted to tell them.

HARVEY ARATON
Montclair, New Jersey
Winter 2001

Prologue

THE MIDDAY SUN shone brightly over the vast acreage of the park's grassy field, where dozens upon dozens of children zigzagged in bright colors and cleats to the tune of British-accented commands. The three-hour camp session was winding down, another morning of work and water, scrimmages and snacks. The caravan of station wagons and sport utility vehicles was coming, the drivers easing their way around the bend of the park and into the makeshift spaces along the curb.

Within weeks, with the coming of the fall colors, the ritual of weekend youth soccer would consume these children and their parents. It would be different then. The mothers and fathers would shout encouragement and ring the field, training their eyes on their own and trying not to be too obvious about it.

Not here, though. Not now. Summer soccer camp was different.

For a parent otherwise unoccupied, the morning camp was a three-hour respite, an invitation to a good novel on the back deck, a coffee date at Starbucks, a workout at the Y. Drop-off at 8:45, collection at noon, no involvement in the process, not even at morning's end. There were too many children to spot one's own, so the mothers and the nannies and the small number of fathers strolled from their cars, some with toddlers or dogs on leashes. They made small talk with friends. They found shady trees to stand under. They planned lunches and maybe a later rendezvous at the community pool.

Except, on this day, for one mother, kicking a ball with her four-year-old daughter at the edge of the field, on the outside looking in.

Her two other children were still with their groups, out in the crowd. Her son was eight, already an elite travel-team player. Her older daughter was six, all arms, legs, and zeal, a ready-made role model for her kid sister.

Sports role models abounded these days for girls. What a time to be young, ponytailed, and light on one's feet. No one knew it better than this particular mother, who was thrilled that her daughters would be growing up with opportunities she never had.

Conversely, she had for some time been feeling pangs of sadness, of frustration, at being little more than a spectator, shackled to the sideline presumably until her kids were finished playing, at which time her connection to team sports would conclude. She hadn't yet articulated this to anyone, even herself, but the more she watched her children, the more she found herself wishing that she could experience that sense of adventure, of freedom, of flying with the wind at her back.

She had played some sports, some high school girls' basketball, what seemed like an eternity ago. Now, in her late thirties, the birth of her children fading in life's rearview mirror, she was once again fit and trim, with a long, purposeful stride.

As it was to most American adults, the soccer ball was a fairly exotic object to her. Before the kids came along, the game had not even been on her radar screen. But here was one soccer mom who loved kicking around, enjoyed sharing her children's passion for the game that seemed to be taking over every park, lawn, and green suburban acre. She had to admit: When she kicked the ball—the proper way, she prided herself, with the instep of her foot—something childlike and joyful stirred inside her. While this might have been an exercise in monotony for every other woman she knew, she couldn't wait to get the ball back, to stride into it again.

Right foot, left foot. She had done some dancing and was used to being on her toes. Either way felt natural. From a distance she looked and moved like an athlete, and on this oppressive August day, the leader of one of the camp groups had noticed.

"That's pretty good," the English trainer said to her, sending back an errant ball with an engaging smile. "Do you play?"

The mother shook her head.

"Too bad," the young man said.

"Too bad," the mother blurted out before she could reconsider, "there's no soccer league for mothers."

Was this a complaint or was it a plea? The trainer, to his credit, heard both.

1

Across the Sideline

L ISA CIARDI was apprehensive that first day. Doubt hovered over her carefully executed plan like an overcast sky. Did she really believe that a handful of women who were preoccupied with work and kids, with leaks and lawns, would have time for what was, to them, a child's game? What would these women, most of whom she barely knew, think of her if they all felt foolish, or inept, trying to dribble a soccer ball? On the other hand, Lisa also wondered if they'd even show up.

She hadn't slept well, waking at her usual time, 5:30. The time before her children stirred, just before her husband would leave for his long commute to Connecticut, was when Lisa could work up a plan, prioritize her day. She could stretch the stiffness out of her chronic back, or "just plain veg, without worrying that anyone would interrupt." Not today, though. Not this bright October morning, when she was infused with unfamiliar energy, counting the minutes until the kids were off to school.

It had been weeks since her chance encounter in the park with Steve Cook, the camp soccer trainer who had taken a moment to comment on her promising form. She considered it serendipity, a stroke of fate. Cook, from Oxford, came from a country that was not receptive to women in sports, and especially not in the sport that mattered most. In a complete reversal of status from the men's game, women's soccer in England was primitive compared with the level it had achieved in the United States. Much like American baseball, the game was bound by deeply rooted traditions and outdated ideals.

But the twenty-seven-year-old Steve Cook had his own, more enlightened views. The first team he ever coached was a group of English women. While going to school in Phoenix, he had guided an under-fourteen girls' team to the Arizona state title. At another stop during his coaching wanderings around the United States, he had bunked for one summer with a family in Troy, Michigan; the mother, Becky Fiedler, was in her forties and had played soccer with several other women her own age for years. "I got the idea that most adult women played here, too," he said. "I actually was surprised when Lisa said there was no place for her to play."

So their first brief exchange became a dialogue that would soon give rise to the beginning of a plan. Lisa would later recall that it was she who had been persistent, who had not dropped the subject; she had taken Steve's compliment, his passing interest, as an open invitation and an offer of help. The way things had gone for the previous twenty years, this might be the only opportunity she would ever get.

Sport already was a dominant presence in her life, given the hours she spent shepherding her three children around to a never-ending swirl of events. John, Lisa's oldest, had just started third grade and was already on travel soccer and hockey teams, playing upward of eighty games from September through May and attending practices three or four times a week. Olivia, a first-grader, was playing soccer in the town recreation league and was in a demanding gymnastics program during the week. Madeline was only four, but in soccer-crazed Montclair that was old enough: Saturday mornings she was one of the kinder kickers learning to dribble around the orange cones and giggling parents over on the south end of town. From the moment Lisa fetched the children at school, the mad rush to get them places on time began.

"I juggle so much it's unbelievable," she said. "The last couple of years, it's been a case of, 'Let's just get through this day.'"

And the weekend was no leisurely affair either. Lisa's husband, Brian, was, weather permitting, a Sunday morning golfer, using the game as a stress-relieving diversion from the grueling hours he was putting in at his securities firm in Greenwich, Connecticut, more than an hour's drive away. When the family considered relocating, the city girl in Lisa was unimpressed by the pricier but more sterile northern suburbs. Brian had grown up about forty-five minutes west of Montclair, where he had spent many afternoons pursuing his true passion, ice hockey, on frozen ponds. He still played in an adult league at the town rink. For Lisa, this was occasionally a source of irritation, as her husband of more than eleven years—bag slung over his shoulder—would leave her alone with the kids.

He would say, "I'm just out there for a couple of hours with a bunch of sweaty guys, just working out." But that was the point: He was, and she wasn't.

All in all, the Ciardis were quite the team sports family, as long as you didn't count Mom. But Lisa wanted to be counted. The more games she watched, the more sidelines she stalked, the more she resented being out of bounds. The occasional tennis game at the Glen Ridge Country Club, the routine aerobics workout at the Y, kept her in good enough shape. At five-five, with a lean, athletic build and naturally dark complexion, she always looked fit. Yet something was missing.

Lisa envied her husband, her children, and everyone else's children. Every season, every week, they had opportunities to free themselves from the stress of school, of work, of the requisite anxieties of their respective ages. To Lisa sports represented adventure, even if they took you no farther than the closest park. They were still an escape, a chance to stay spiritually young. She wanted to have that connection to childhood, to make that leap back in time to the streets of Bay Ridge, Brooklyn, when her mother would look out the window and cringe as Lisa, fast on her feet and unafraid, was usually leaping for a football, slamming into a parked car.

Neither her mother nor her father, a doctor, endorsed sports. They stressed academics for their five children. In fact, when Lisa's mother was thirty-seven, the same age as her daughter was now, she had gone back to school for a master's in education. Lisa already had a master's degree; she had enough education. But now, with all three of her children about to be in school full-time, she, too, felt she needed something else.

"I spoke to my mother about it. She said, 'When I got to your age, I needed something for myself. The kids were beyond the infant stage, and I'd done a lot of things for my family. I started to think, What can I do now that's just for me?'"

Lisa was not yet ready to return to her work as a physical therapist, which she had left after her second child came along. Brian was working long hours, and the children were too young, adjusting to school and academics and all those after-school activities. Lisa had shepherded them through the diaper and toddler years. Now the long-dormant jock in her was crying out for some playtime of her own.

"I always wanted to be out there, with the boys, playing every sport," she said. "I always knew I was an athletic person. When I played sports, I'd put everything into it. I like to run. I like to sweat, work hard. I always loved the boy things. I always played like a boy. To be honest, I always felt I should have been a boy, except I wanted to have kids."

In 1970s Brooklyn few people paid much attention to the distant hum of Title IX. Lisa was growing up in the age of feminism, of Gloria Steinem and cigarette commercials that told her that she'd come a long way, baby. But how far was that, when it came to sports?

The neighborhood boys she competed with had places to take their street passions. They could go off to play the team sport they excelled at and enjoyed. They'd get a uniform, a schedule. Fathers lined up, volunteering to coach. Even if an athletic girl had enlightened parents, she usually had to find more acceptable pursuits.

When Lisa was thirteen she bounded off a trampoline, landing too hard on her feet. Her spinal column was never quite the same. She would, after several years of pain, undergo back surgery at sixteen, then again at twenty-one. At Notre Dame Academy, a high school for girls across the Verrazano-Narrows Bridge in Staten Island, Lisa won a few medals running track. She tried a little basketball, but none of this moved her. Her back often hurt, and sports were not even on her friends' radar screens. Before Lisa knew it she was at New York University, studying psychology and biology, getting her master's in physical therapy. Her athletic ambitions were more or less numbed into submission by peer pressure—or lack of same—and societal indifference. She never did find her way back to the street, until her own children led her into the park.

A FTER HIS CHAT with Lisa, Steve Cook went to Ashley Hammond, owner and operator of the camp and other youth programs in and around Montclair. Hammond, a British expatriate, imported much of his staff from England, hiring young coaches, men and women, on short-term contracts. Ashley was the center of the Montclair soccer universe, arguably the most influential sportsperson in town. He had settled in the area about a decade earlier, having come from Essex County, England, to Essex County, New Jersey. He was in his early twenties back then, a highly skilled player whose own promising pro soccer career was short-circuited by injuries. Now his summer camps were practically a rite of passage for local five-year-olds. His company had taken over the operation of all the elite travel teams in several towns, including Montclair. When he became coach of Montclair Kimberley, a small, private academy, he created a regional power that was competitive with the much larger local public school.

Ashley and his partner, Glen Pernia, were astute, aggressive entrepreneurs, but their success in American suburbia was rooted in the child-friendly environment they had created at their camps. Hundreds of kids, a fair number on scholarship, passed through every summer, and many more participated in their travel team programs in spring and fall. Ashley seemed to know everyone by name, and often by particular skills as well.

He knew Lisa because her children, especially John, were camp regulars. But when Steve Cook broached the subject of a training session for moms, and Lisa followed up with her own request, Ashley was skeptical. He wondered if Lisa was an aberration, preaching for a congregation that did not exist. "Get me a list of names," he told her, "and we'll see if we can put something together."

Lisa accepted the challenge—though not immediately, because she knew that in August, with the humidity soaring, it was all the mothers could do some mornings to get their kids to kick a ball under the burning sun. Half the town was off to the shore, if not long gone from North Jersey. September would be a better time to make connections. Lisa's children attended three different schools, and they would all be playing soccer; dozens of mothers would be exactly where they always were, right alongside her on the sideline. "I decided to scout out a certain type, women who looked athletic," she said. "Sometimes you could just tell."

She began with one woman whom she knew casually from school pickup and who was typically rushing off in workout clothes, presumably to the Y. Her name was Dana. One September day Lisa took a deep breath and approached her. "You work out all the time. Would you be interested in playing soccer?"

Dana DiMuro didn't quite know what to say. Soccer? Her husband, Declan, had played growing up in Ireland; all she had ever done athletically, beyond workouts, was smack a few balls against school yard walls in the Bronx. Her knowledge of soccer was pretty much limited to Pelé and kinder kickers. "Sure," she blurted out, without giving it much thought. "Why not?"

Lisa felt as if she was off the starting line, in business. Another woman she knew fairly well from the school, Clare Moore, said she was interested, too. On the one hand, Clare, thirty-six, did not fit the category of the "Un-Titled Woman": someone too old to have been affected by Title IX, or just not lucky enough to have stumbled into one sport or another. She grew up in Scotland, outside Edinburgh, playing field hockey and net ball, a variation of basketball. On the other hand, as she put it, "I haven't had any real exercise for years." She told Lisa, "I've never kicked a ball in my life, but if it'll get me in better shape, put me down."

Lisa was encouraged, energized, and surprised at her ability to be so forward. She had never considered herself much of an organizer or leader. Her personality included a fairly obvious element of shyness; she often waited for others to make eye contact. She knew most of these women only in the context of picking up the kids, or assisting the teacher for a class party or trip. Sometimes they'd have a casual conversation, and sometimes not.

Another mother from the nursery school had noticed that Lisa would sometimes brush past without a word or nod. Ellen Paretti knew Lisa was from Montclair, while Ellen lived in Bloomfield, a more dressed-down community on Montclair's eastern flank. Some adolescent and stereotypical notions about economic and social rank we never quite lose, and Ellen had no way of knowing that Lisa, more times than not, was rushing by to make sure she didn't wind up with a child waiting for her in tears at another end of town. One day Ellen looked up at the school bulletin board and saw a notice about women wanted for a beginners' soccer group. Anyone interested should contact Lisa Ciardi.

Ellen's husband, Andy, had played the game. She used to watch him from the sideline early in their relationship. Now the older of her two boys had started to play. Not once in her life had Ellen played anything resembling a team sport. She occasionally jogged—which she thought of as work, not play—and generally considered herself, athletically speaking, "a klutz."

Ellen had also been looking for something new to try, though she hadn't really given much thought to what that something might be. When she asked Lisa about soccer, something about Lisa's absolute seriousness caught her attention. Lisa might as well have been talking about a mothers' playgroup, or book club, something no one would have thought the least bit odd. Lisa's earnestness stirred memories for Ellen, of standing around as a kid, watching neighborhood boys in nearby Bergen County play baseball and basketball. Of thinking that someday, somehow, she might like to join in. "I've always, you know, wanted to be an athlete," she said.

Lisa added Ellen Paretti's name to her list.

At the Bradford School, where Olivia was starting first grade, Lisa marched to the rear of the building, to find the parents waiting for their children. There she approached more mothers, collected more names: Ginger Steuart, who had just moved to town from

Brooklyn and whose husband, Henry, was an absolute soccer fanatic. Beth Albert, the PTA president, whose son had been in John's first-grade class, said she might give it a try. So did Beth Fuqua, whose kindergartner, Jeffrey, was already declaring soccer the greatest sport ever invented. She fancied the thought of mother and son sharing something athletic.

By the end of September, Lisa had twenty-four names. She returned to Ashley Hammond, who looked at the list and noticed something else: The women had written down not only their names but specific times they would be available. Ashley looked at that and thought, Maybe we're on to something.

Flyers offering a four-week, fifty-dollar course were printed, with the imprimatur of Ashley's Soccer Camp. "I was surprised, pleasantly surprised, when he came on board," Lisa said. "I figured more women would try it, because his camps had so much credibility in the community."

Steve Cook agreed to train the women, and Ashley assigned David Law, another of his British imports, to assist. Lisa went on a one-woman mission to post the flyers at schools, distribute them at games, supermarkets, Starbucks, wherever she thought mothers might see them. Having made the list, Lisa was now checking it twice. She called Ellen Paretti, who wanted to play but did not have a sitter. Lisa said she would see what she could do. She called back in a few days. "I talked to everyone I know, and I finally found someone for you," she said.

Nine dollars an hour was definitely a Montclair price. Ellen eventually tracked down her own sitter, but what stayed with her was her amazement at Lisa's sheer resolve. "I remember thinking, She must really want this to happen to make such an effort for someone else," Ellen said.

Lisa's posse of eighteen women came to the side of Brookdale Park that was actually across the border, in Bloomfield, on the morning of October 21. They didn't really know what they were getting themselves into. They were all mothers, most of them active in some kind of recreation. Soccer? Nobody on the list had ever played beyond a few kicks with the kids. They all had come, however, with the same motivational mantra as Dana DiMuro: Why not? It looked like fun. What was stopping them from giving it a try?

That Wednesday morning they assembled for the first time, some in cleats, a few in sneakers. They came carrying coffee cups, giggling at each other as they made their way from the parking lot across the field. Ginger Steuart pushed three-year-old Gwendolyn in her stroller. When she reached the familiar sight of an area marked by orange cones, she placed a white blanket over her daughter, handed her a small box of crackers, and gave her a kiss. "Mommy will be right over there," she said. She pointed to where Steve Cook and David Law were calling for the "ladies" to stretch before a ball would be dropped at their feet. It was a beautiful autumn morning, cloudless and crisp.

Lisa wasn't nervous anymore. She didn't feel silly. Much to the contrary, she felt strong, independent, proud. "This is my turn," she would recall thinking as she loosened up, not far from where Steve Cook only weeks before had noticed her natural athleticism and told her, "That's pretty good." This was, in fact, better than good. What Lisa would most remember from that first day was how great it felt to actually be on the playing field, across the sideline, and the invisible divide.

2

Town and Country

O N MOST FALL and spring weekends the township of
Montclair looked like many other affluent bedroom
communities, with its postcard Colonials and rambling
Victorians, lush parks, and familiar array of upscale vehicles toting
children to and from their soccer games. A closer inspection, however, reveals something different. Montclair is no cookie-cutter
suburb where homogeneity rules. In fact, many Montclairians considered themselves to be living in the middle of a grand social
experiment, a town of approximately 38,000 that they felt was cast
in the image of the megalopolis roughly twelve miles and one river-
crossing to the east.

Like New York City, Montclair prides itself on its racial and
socioeconomic diversity. More than 30 percent of the town's population is African American, and since the 1970s children had been

bused to integrated schools that were nationally heralded—though in recent budget-strained years, more for progressive intentions.

On a ride through town one could motor past châteaulike mansions with stunning city views that were only minutes away from grinding poverty. Though there was a clear delineation between neighborhoods that were more or less affluent, and blacker or whiter, there were African Americans living in every part of town. There had traditionally been a lower percentage of whites at the public middle and high schools, but those numbers, eyed warily, appeared stable. There was little sign of the white flight that often created only transitional urban diversity.

At its best Montclair was a contentious place of preferred coexistence. For the New York metropolitan area, especially during the real estate ultraboom of the late 1990s, it became something of a hotbed for liberal professionals, both black and white, who were reluctantly leaving the city for additional space and better public schools. They poured into town from the row houses and brownstones of Brooklyn and Hoboken, and from all over Manhattan.

With its tall, handsome trees standing guard like sentinels, Montclair provided little open space in town for developers to exploit. The town boasted an array of ethnic restaurants, an impressive art museum, a state university, a variety of music venues, storefronts catering to coffee sippers and poets, local theater companies, and art movie houses. Yet for all the pastoral beauty that made it a perfect location for production companies shooting commercials and feature films, Montclair was also definitively urban. It had its own civil rights commission, and a political system that divided the town into old-fashioned urban wards much like Newark, the troubled city close by to the south.

Montclair was sometimes referred to as the urban suburb. With its reputation for tolerance the town had become attractive to biracial couples, families that had adopted children of different nationality or color, and gay and lesbian couples. Though many Wall Street types and executives lugged briefcases to train stations and bus stops, scores of television and print journalists, novelists, artists, and actors had settled in Montclair as well.

During the 1990s one could walk into a coffee shop and sit in a booth opposite any number of performers of stage and screen, from Savion Glover to Joe Morton, Olympia Dukakis to Christina Ricci. Bill Bradley was a regular on the treadmill at the Park Street Y until he took off on the presidential campaign trail. Yogi Berra was typically holding court at the new museum and child learning center named in his honor on the Montclair State University campus. Baseball Hall of Famer Larry Doby lived on the town's south side.

On any given weekend at an independent bookstore, one of the town's resident authors, a Valerie Wilson Wesley or an Alice Elliott Dark, might be reading from her latest work of fiction. Frankie Faison, a Tony nominee for *Fences,* might be performing at the Luna Stage. The Grammy Award–winning jazz artist Geri Allen might be playing with her band at Trumpet's. The soap opera star Kim Zimmer of *Guiding Light* or the makeup artist and mogul Bobbi Brown might be found yelling encouragement on the sideline at her children's soccer games.

In November 1996 the pride of Montclair's city transplants swelled along with their house values as *New York* magazine dubbed the town "the Upper West Side of New Jersey." Three years later, in the November 7, 1999, issue of *The New York Times Magazine* a story titled "Integration Anxiety" noted that "Montclair has embraced racial diversity like no other town in America."

"Race is a part of every conversation in this town," said Jessica de Koninck, a white town council member. Strangely enough one place it wasn't talked about much was on the soccer fields, where it was plainly evident that the players were overwhelmingly white.

The argument could have been made that the expense of a child playing on a travel team, several hundred dollars a year, may have exceeded the means of many of the working-class black families in town. There were scholarships available, however, and the town recreational leagues charged the same nominal sum that other programs more representative of the town's ethnic makeup cost.

Ashley Hammond believed the explanation might have more to do with the way many Americans view soccer in the first place. "Americans, especially in the suburbs, see it as an alternative to football, which they think is violent and dangerous, unsafe for their children, even if they enjoy watching it on television," he said. According to his reasoning, it didn't make sense for people of means to insulate their suburban children from societal ills and then encourage them to beat the hell out of one another on the football field. Yet football was popular in Montclair; the high school team was a county powerhouse, usually with a majority of black players. When the Parks & Recreation Department started a football league for boys ten through thirteen in September 1999, that league looked nothing like the town's soccer fields.

The "soccer versus football" dynamic in Montclair raised a debate similar to the one that ensued when ROTC was introduced at the high school during the mid-1990s. Some white liberals argued against a military presence, claiming it was divisive, segregationist, a way to avoid dealing with underachieving children from poor or dysfunctional homes. Many of the families that supported the predominantly black ROTC program were not inherently pro-military; they argued that their at-risk children needed discipline and direction, and that ROTC might provide it.

Few people in Montclair ever mentioned those rewards as they related to soccer. Teamwork, fair play; when the game ends, apple juice and cookies for all. This was what early youth soccer represented to upscale Montclair, until a child began to demonstrate some serious skills and the proud parents began to entertain thoughts of a potential, albeit unlikely, college scholarship.

Soccer was the safe alternative, the sensible way for a suburban child of middle-class or affluent means to work up a good sweat. In the aftermath of Title IX, mothers who had never played sports and overprotective fathers thought of soccer as an acceptable game for their little girls. Ashley believed that is why women's soccer took off here before it did anywhere else, certainly long before it even began to draw participatory interest in England.

Anna Girdwood, one of the women's coaches Ashley had hired from England, was stunned when she arrived for her first summer camp. There were four large groups made up entirely of girls. "Back home, if there was a group of a hundred kids, there was maybe a total of three girls," she said. Anna, twenty-four, had grown up in a small town, playing pickup games with the boys who would soon join leagues. There were none for her, and she wasn't allowed to play in the boys' leagues, either.

Even now, compared with England, America was a land of pony-tailed opportunity. But Anna and Karen Sherris, another of the English girls' coaches, also realized that Americans were just beginning to acknowledge that the game—generally speaking, and particularly for young girls—was something much more intense than simply recreational fun. It was not, as Anna said, just "letting the kids get out there to kick the ball around with as little contact as possible."

Anyone raised in Europe understands that soccer is very much a contact sport, a dangerous game of hurtling bodies, played without helmets and pads. Americans were just catching on, and starting to wonder, for example, what the effects might be from having a soccer ball crash repeatedly off a child's noggin.

Ashley, recalling a tournament game his Montclair Kimberley team had played against a rival school, remembered it being so physical that it was akin to "wanton violence." He went so far as to call the game, in Europe especially, the sporting equivalent of continental conflict. "Since the 1940s, other than the Balkans, it's been the tribal nature of soccer stadiums that has generated warlike fever there," he said. "It's all very clannish. We have it here, in the American sports, too. I've never been to Yankee Stadium and not seen a fight."

He did not espouse or teach dirty or violent play. He just wanted to be clear about the fact that soccer, played correctly and competitively, is no gentlemanly sport, no croquet. If you wanted to be a serious player, you had better be dedicated, willing to play fall and spring schedules, and to practice in between. When baseball organizers in Montclair complained that soccer was limiting the choices for many children, Ashley pointed out that soccer is a year-round activity worldwide. Kids who wanted to be tennis players or gymnasts have to make early commitments; that was what it was going to take, in most cases, to play soccer, too, even just on the competitive scholastic level.

He considered it an insult when the advocates of the more traditional American games suggested that soccer was not as important or intense. In teaching the game to children in the States, Ashley had naturally been forced to embrace some of the country's suburban etiquette. Most Americans, for example, were adamant that, once a child was on a team, he or she was entitled to as much playing time as anyone; that went against the traditional soccer grain. In England, Ashley said, children were trained to play the whole game; substitutions were tactical, rare, and often only because of injury.

But the game was the game. It was strenuous. It was rough. It was fierce. It was more work than the typical American parent could ever imagine, until he or she walked out on that field.

• • •

WITH AN EDUCATIONAL background in sports physiology, Steve Cook worried about his newest team, the soccer moms, and their reactions to the difficulty of the simplest drills. When he demonstrated the basic step-up—foot up on the ball, down, other foot up, down—the strain on the muscles was evident from the many pained faces. "It became clear that the first goal we had to have was to help the women get into better shape using the fundamental soccer drills," he said. "Most of them were in decent shape, as far as running. But there's a big difference between that and playing a sport, with all the stopping and starting and changing of direction."

That first day, Beth Fuqua, thirty-eight, suffered the unceremonious first spraining of the ankle. She had worn sneakers, not bothering to purchase cleats because she didn't know if her soccer career would extend beyond one morning. While running, attempting to cut, she slipped. She limped home and telephoned the youngest of her three kid brothers, to whom she had become something of a big brother after the death of their father when she was sixteen and he was eight. "I was a girlie girl," she said, of her childhood in suburban Detroit. "But when our father died, I found myself doing more boy things."

Her first sports-related injury! Now she had a real "boy-thing" to brag about to David, who still played and coached soccer at his home in Virginia.

She was better by the following week, but her friend Beth Albert had to be helped home after badly straining her quadricep muscle, at the front of the thigh. Still, all she needed was a week or two to rest and heal. Poor Marcia Kramer wound up in the orthopedist's office and under anesthesia to repair torn cartilage. Her soccer career over, she went on to something she felt was significantly safer: rock climbing. Meanwhile, Ginger Steuart was having a great time kicking the ball, except for when her trick knee—the result of massive ligament damage suffered two decades before while skiing at Squaw Valley—began to throb.

The physical demands of even a few soccer drills were taking their toll. The number of attending moms dropped from eighteen at the first week's ninety-minute session to an average of about twelve for the remaining three weeks. Lisa, relishing every minute, sensed a growing bond among the core women as they limbered up and generally drove Steve and Dave crazy with their nonstop chatter and their inability to obey the trainers, who ordered them to stop apologizing for bumping into one another.

"Sorry."

"Oops."

Then came the apologies for apologizing, usually followed by an outburst of laughter.

They were having a ball, yet Lisa worried how long the group would last. Her insomnia on the nights before soccer practice continued. It was obvious to her by now that if they were going to really learn, really play, they needed the trainers' expertise. She wondered how much of a window they had to convince Ashley it was worth his while to carry on.

By the fourth and last session, unbeknownst to Lisa, he had been sold. On a wet, dreary day Ashley stood on the side and watched as Steve and Dave paced the women through the drills. "I'm stunned, actually," he said, as they called out to one another for passes, stopped the ball with the side of one foot, transferred it to the other, and sent it off in another direction. They played a four-goal scrimmage, in which four sets of cones are left unguarded and a goal is scored when one team member passes to another through the cones. It looked like, well, a scrimmage.

"What's obvious is that they are picking things up quickly, the way kids tend to, no matter what it is they're being taught," Ashley said. "And it's obvious that they are enjoying this, moving from the loneliness of the Y to doing something together."

They couldn't help but judge themselves according to adult

expectations, though, especially Lisa. To the others she was clearly the best, the fastest and most focused. "She had that extra edge," said Susan Hatzopoulos. "It was like she was one with the ball, like it was stuck to her foot."

Lisa, apparently in a hurry to make up for lost time, still didn't think she was mastering the game fast enough. "I was a little turned off at first," she said. "I'd go in my basement and try to do one of the moves, a drag-back turn. I'd try to visualize what Steve or David had taught us. Slowly, I began to realize it was just relaxing and feeling comfortable, getting used to the foot on the ball. And that all these things in time would come."

When the last session was over, Ashley announced that they would have more time. "If anything," he said, gathering the women around, "I think you all have a better appreciation of how hard this is for your children." He passed around applications for the next multiweek session of what he was now promoting as Soccer Moms in Training.

In training for what? Nobody was certain about that yet. But Ashley had seen enough to know there was something worth pursuing here, something fresh, original, and if he hadn't figured this out for himself, there was one soccer-playing mom who had helped him along. Her name was Meg Goor, soon to be Mrs. Ashley Hammond.

WHEN MEG WAS a seventeen-year-old high school senior, she was directing a play, practicing scenes with her friends one day in a nearby park. She had climbed up on a friend's shoulder when typical teenage horseplay turned near tragic. She fell awkwardly, about eighteen inches, and landed on her head.

"Don't move, don't move," her friends shouted, as she lay there, dazed, thinking just the opposite. She had heard and felt a terrifying snap. All she could tell herself was, "Move! Move!" She sat up but could not raise her arms, could not remove the turtleneck sweater she was wearing on that cool November day.

Upon being driven home and feeling agony when the car hit the smallest bump, she was rushed to the local hospital. A lab technician ordered her to remove her earrings. Her arms would not obey, would not move at all. X rays soon disclosed massive swelling and apparent fractures and dislocations to the C-5 and C-6 vertebrae. "Within minutes they had me down, out, sandbagged, lifted out to another hospital," she said. "By that time my whole right side was gone. I couldn't move it at all. They weren't even sure if I was going to live because everything was swelling so much."

Twenty years later Meg could look back at that life-altering event and consider herself lucky. She had grown up in Freeport, Long Island, listening to the soothing sound of the waves crashing onto Jones Beach. Freeport was still Jets football territory, from the years when they had played at Shea Stadium in Queens; if Meg could compare her injury to anyone's, it was that of the Jets defensive lineman Dennis Byrd, whose career ended suddenly, violently, after a 1992 collision at Giants Stadium in New Jersey.

Byrd walked again after initial paralysis, because, doctors contended, treatment had been swift and sure. After three months in a halo and eight more weeks in a collar, Meg regained the movement in her right side. But the injury extracted a long-term price: The vertebrae eventually had to be fused, which the doctors accomplished by taking bone from her hip. The trauma had created symptoms similar to those of a stroke, and there was permanent nerve damage. She would require years of isometrics, therapy, and ongoing rehabilitation.

After her recovery Meg went to the Fashion Institute of Technology to learn drafting and later became an artist. The work took its toll. "Torture," she called it.

By the time she was in her late thirties, a divorced mother of three children between twelve and eight, she had started weight training and had become a regular at the Park Street Y. If she didn't work out, her right side would atrophy, and fast. She would develop a noticeable limp, and simple chores like extended cooking, or writing out the invitations to her coming wedding, would become an ordeal.

As a single mother Meg had for several years been dropping her kids off at Ashley's Soccer Camp without even knowing which one was Ashley. She would pull up to the curb, where a smiling teenager would open the door. *Ball? Check. Water bottles? Check. Have a great day. See you at noon.*

Ashley had been through a failed, childless marriage since arriving in Montclair. But when a mutual friend introduced them, Meg said to herself, "He has no kids. He's thinking, 'What is this going to be like?'" But in his line of work, Ashley—animal lover and vegetarian—had to adore kids, especially those old enough to kick a soccer ball. And now Meg and Ashley were just weeks away from their wedding day.

For all her dedication to her weight training regimen, Meg needed something to break up the tedium. The usual alternative exercise, jogging, was never an option; she hated the routine, the isolation. When a friend, Paul Friedman, created a circuit training program for the high school team Ashley was coaching, Meg gave it a try. There she was, sweating her way through the rigorous drills with a bunch of muscular seventeen-year-olds. "It was intimidating," she said, but it was wonderful being outdoors, in the park. It gave her the idea that perhaps she and Ashley could create an alternative workout for women, something removed from the stuffiness of the Y.

"In looking at it from a business point of view, we had already been talking about something," she said. "An intense aerobic activity, rather than endurance, a five-mile run. I hadn't looked at it from the standpoint of playing soccer, but more of a training regimen, because that's what I needed out of it."

Then one day Ashley mentioned Lisa Ciardi's desire to create the soccer mom's group. Meg was intrigued; she knew the stretching, lateral movement, and sprinting would be therapeutic, perfect for her. There was one problem: she was right-footed. "I'll tell my leg, 'Move,' and it doesn't," she said. "I really have to think about it, concentrate, because my response is much slower on my right side. But that's what makes soccer so good for me. The harder I concentrate on using the muscles, the stronger they are."

Much like Lisa, Meg had grown up tussling with boys, her lacrosse-playing brothers, who made her stand in the goal while they used her for backyard target practice. Freeport was a big sports town of large Irish Catholic families, where the boys were steered to the sports fields and the girls to the sidelines.

Meg loved sports, though, and always had. She would keep meticulous box scores while listening to the Yankees and the Mets on the radio. She would go to her brothers' lacrosse games, and their baseball games, too, and she went with her father and brothers to watch the Jets train at Hofstra and the Giants over at C. W. Post. Saturday afternoons she and her father would sit on the couch watching pro bowlers like Earl Anthony. Her dad had always bowled, Wednesday nights, in competitive leagues; as Meg came of age, she did, too. The high school had few sports for girls, but it did have a bowling team.

"You mention bowling now and people are like, 'You what?'" Meg said. But back in Freeport it was a way—the only way, as far as she remembered—that father and daughter could make that connection, that wonderful sports connection, same as the guys'.

Meg had played softball for a few years not long after she moved to Montclair. It was a good way to get out of the house on spring and summer evenings, socialize, and let the kids work off some steam. She was on a team with women in their thirties and forties, some of whom were just getting familiar with the intricacies of the game, such as, Where's second base?

"The other teams had women in their twenties who had grown up playing," she said. "They hated us. The umps hated us because we couldn't play, and our kids were running all over the field. They had that five-inning rule, down by fifteen and the game gets called. Our games always lasted an hour. It took us three years to win a game. We beat Petrella Paving. Petrella was always our best game. They'd show up with cigarettes dangling from their lips and wearing construction boots. We'd be taking off our jewelry. It was hysterical, so much fun. The camaraderie was the best part. I stopped playing when the kids started having their own games and practices. I missed it. When Ashley told me about the soccer, I knew right away I wanted to try."

Meg did not know Lisa, though they both had boys in third grade. They had a few other things in common: They were roughly the same age, both had four siblings and now three children of their own. But there were differences, superficial and otherwise. While Meg was blond, Lisa was dark. Meg had a breezy, congenial air about her, while Lisa came across as more private, cautious. But while they came to soccer for vastly different reasons, they would both one day be able to look back and see how prominently soccer had figured in redirecting their lives, in rearranging their values and goals. For now they were unlikely compatriots taking halting steps toward their goals, an unfamiliar ball at their feet.

3

Soul of a Soccer Mom

WHEN HER THREE BOYS were all under five, Susan Hatzopoulos got a valuable piece of parenting advice from a reliable voice of experience. Her aunt, who had already raised a trio of males, suggested that she develop an interest in sports, preferably team sports. This, Susan was told, was a surefire way of maintaining common ground with the boys as they approached adolescence and retreated from those halcyon years of communication and cuddling. There would, presumably, always be a game to watch.

Susan thus set out to learn sports with better parenting in mind, and wound up with a serious basketball Jones. It was not because she had played, or because she happened to be tall, a centimeter short of five-eight. In the way Lisa Ciardi seemed to have naturally taken to soccer, Susan became riveted by the magnificence of Michael Jordan.

She rooted hard for the determined but socially dysfunctional Knicks. She was intoxicated by their fierce play-off games.

Susan was athletic and extremely energetic herself. Approaching forty, she had trained for her first marathon with her friend Cathy Wright, who had by this time finished more than twenty and had once been nationally ranked as a supermarathoner. Susan covered the New York City course in four hours, forty-three minutes, long after Cathy had finished, but considered this one of the achievements she was most proud of. Better yet, her longest run convinced her there were more victories to come, calendar be damned.

She loved curling up on a winter night with the boys and her husband, Arthur, and flipping on a game from Madison Square Garden. The house males relentlessly teased her when the 1998–99 NBA season was delayed three months by an acrimonious lockout and she scoured the newspapers for signs of a settlement. She took the lockout hard but the ribbing in the good-natured way it was meant.

Jim, David, and Peter, ranging in grade from fifth down to first, actually thought it was cool that their mother could talk sports. But as Susan soon and sadly learned, not every male welcomed her input. Particularly deflating was an attempt to contribute one day to a basketball conversation with two local men. The two men smiled, nodded, and continued talking.

When it happened again, Susan pressed the issue, wondering out loud what the problem was. One of the men, in a startlingly matter-of-fact manner, made himself perfectly clear: Not only did he think women didn't belong in the middle of his male-bonding conversation but he didn't believe they had a place in team sports either.

While the latter opinion could almost—not quite—be dismissed on the grounds that it was patently absurd, or just a tease, the former touched a sensitive nerve. "Here I was, a forty-year-old woman, a colleague, and reasonably educated on the subject that they were discussing, and it was as if I was invisible," she said. Susan understood the score too well; those men could have been talking about lacrosse, linens, or Lyme disease. She just wasn't welcome, and she understood part of the reason why. "We—women getting near and into their forties—begin to become invisible, to fade away," she said.

As a former booking agent for models at *Self* magazine, Susan was something of an expert on the ogling habits of older men. When they were neighbors in Greenwich Village, Susan was introduced to her husband by Bobbi Brown, whose meteoric rise as a makeup mogul had resulted from spit-shining those very models (and eventually the likes of Susan Sarandon and Brooke Shields).

Bobbi, of all people, could relate. All of five feet tall, she enjoyed telling the story of when she was pregnant with the first of her three sons and happened to be in the middle of a shoot that featured Cindy Crawford and Naomi Campbell. "Here I was, feeling fat and ugly, and I'm around these 'perfect' looking women," she said. "But at that moment I made myself a promise that I would never live my own life with those standards, or compare myself with them. There was just no point."

A sports fanatic herself, Bobbi had attended a soccer moms' clinic, but her back hurt afterward, and she decided the risk of having her business affected by injury wasn't worth it. Still, she loved driving around Montclair on weekends, seeing all the fathers rushing into the park with their daughters in bright-colored shirts. When the U.S. Women's World Cup celebrities became her clients, she made a point of telling Mia, Brandi, and Julie how much she wished she had had that same chance.

In the meantime, while working on her best-selling book for teenage girls, Bobbi was contemplating another for women over forty, her generation. For women who were juggling marriages, kids, and careers and who didn't have much time or even the inclination to look in the mirror and admire themselves. Society, Susan Hatzopoulos said, was too often telling them not to bother.

"We can be pretty but we're no longer beautiful," she said. "We're not young mothers anymore, so we're not special in that way either. If we have kids, and we've made sacrifices in our careers to raise them, we're not looked at as big, successful achievers. Sometimes you listen to the way men talk about and act around younger women, the way Hollywood portrays them and older men who always want them, and you just want to say: 'Hello, hel . . . lo. We're still here.'

"And that's why soccer, I believe, felt so good for all of us when we first got out there. It was exercise, but not for the purpose of looking good for anyone else. It was for us, individually and as a group of women with so much in common."

Out on the field they were no longer graying (or soon-to-be) sideline ornaments. They were taking control of their bodies at a time when inevitable menopausal effects were reminding them that every woman's body has a midlife plan all its own. They were not the contemporary female suburban stereotype, the Volvo-driving demographic sorority trying to decide what candidates to help steer to Washington and which cupcakes to contribute to the bake sale.

On the subject of women and political sport, an unnamed "top Republican strategist" was quoted in an October 24, 1999, *New York Times* column by Maureen Dowd related to Hillary Clinton's candidacy for the New York Senate seat: "It's been a longtime secret among political consultants that women hate women candidates," the strategist said. "It's the old thing: You get twelve guys, you've got a football team. You get twelve women, you've got a riot."

Left unmentioned here were the scant number of female candidates, the few potential choices. But the sadder and less enlightened commentary was the strategist's contention that women are only "bred to compete" against one another, and are not inclined to act in the spirit of cooperation and teamwork. Which, of course, was another way of saying that women don't have the capability to empower themselves and consequently face an eternity of being at the mercy of men.

When this piece was published, only three months had passed since the U.S. Women's World Cup soccer team had rewritten the rules of American spectator sports and created a very different kind of jock-ethic metaphor. Myths and habits are tough to kick, though: *Sports Illustrated*'s Athletes of the Year at the turn of the century had to boycott a tournament to get the U.S. Soccer Federation to cough up salaries that were at least close to those of the Federation's thoroughly undistinguished men's team. It was clear that the old-school values remained deeply ingrained in the minds of many, and the soccer-playing mothers were about to discover why, in a very public way.

I N NOVEMBER 1998, *The New York Times* ran a story on the Montclair women, and the phones began ringing at Ashley's Soccer Camp. Women from Montclair and nearby towns were eager to sign up. Overnight, new faces were on the field with the regulars of the Wednesday morning group. Suddenly endowed with a new, invigorating business opportunity, Ashley quickly arranged night clinics in a local gymnasium for those who couldn't play on weekday mornings.

Something was happening that neither Ashley nor Lisa could possibly have imagined—not this fast, anyway. There was a buzz in the community, and that was before the television crews came, one after another. First out was the local NBC news affiliate, led by the sports reporter and weekend anchor Bruce Beck.

On a chilly, overcast day, his report from Brookdale Park began with one of the new players, Nina Sloan, wearing the odd combination of blue jeans and cleats while leading her first-grader, Sam, down the steps of the Rand Public School. "We're used to seeing mothers picking up their kids at school and taking them to and from soccer practice," Beck began. "But in Montclair, New Jersey, things are changing. . . ."

Cut to Lisa, exiting her white minivan and trying—unsuccessfully—to hold back a smile.

"Women are arriving at practice on their own."

The report was cheerfully positive, with Ashley recounting how the group had formed. Lisa wasn't named as the inspirational source, but she wasn't left on the cutting room floor, either. There was a shot of her during a scrimmage, on a breakaway with Meg, with Meg scoring a goal. In a sound bite of her own, Lisa said, "I understand the game better. Most parents will yell from the sideline—'Run, kick the ball.' Now we know how hard it is."

In the spirit of the feel-good evening news feature, most people, including the principals, regarded this as well-intentioned, at worst, benign. Most of these women were not publicity seekers, and they had no carefully crafted agenda. But some were not particularly media savvy and were unaccustomed to having microphones thrust in their faces; they were flattered by the attention, even if these reports tended to pander to stereotypes.

"It gets you out of the house, instead of sitting home, baking," Ellen Paretti said when asked what she liked best about her new pastime. She regretted the statement almost as soon as the words were out of her mouth. It was television, though, and it was too late.

The superficiality of the report wasn't necessarily the fault of Bruce Beck—or Judy Licht, the unfailingly buoyant WABC-TV *Eyewitness News* reporter who several weeks later slipped into a soccer moms' T-shirt and took some inspirational kicks for the viewers at home. It was just what the producers wanted, what the time allotment called for: a few precious Kathie Lee moments. "I know I'm losing weight without dieting," Rochelle Sandler told Licht. While weight loss might have been a welcome by-product, it wasn't necessarily why Rochelle, at forty-five, had taken up soccer.

In a more realistic forum that allowed for a well-rounded answer, this is what she said: "I suddenly found myself approaching a crossroads in my life, trying to fill gaps in the day and an emotional void. My father recently died, and now both of my parents are gone. My two young sons are in school now, full-time. And my daughter from a previous marriage is just a few months away from going off to college. We got through some difficult times together; we have always been very close. The last few years, I took dancing with Becky, jazz and tap. I know it's going to be over when she leaves, though. It's something we shared, and I know I wouldn't do it without her. It would make me miss her even more. My work in interior design and architecture has always afforded me a flexible schedule and time for myself during the day. So I was looking for something new to do; I had always enjoyed walking, jogging, putting the headphones on. I had never done anything competitive with other women. But being with the other women—something just drew me into it and held me. I didn't realize I had this competitive side that was dormant all these years."

While Rochelle was one of the older players, she was hardly the only player with thoughtful and complex reasons to want to play. Beth Panucci turned thirty-three not long after her first soccer clinic; her mother presented her with her first pair of cleats, saying she was thrilled to see her daughter, raised with four brothers who had always played sports, finally getting a chance. "I could see myself doing this for a very long time, if I don't get hurt badly," Beth said. "My mother has very bad rheumatoid arthritis. It's been very painful, very difficult for her, and for us to see her suffer. And with two young daughters, I worry about the hereditary nature of the disease. I've always been active, busy. I got my MBA and was a banker for ten years at J. P. Morgan. I got my aggression in business from my father.

But I worry about my mother's disease, and I feel like I have to do something, stay in condition, keep moving."

This kind of multidimensional profile of the soccer mom was, unfortunately, nowhere to be found in the television features, or in the front-page living-section story that soon appeared in the *Star-Ledger,* New Jersey's largest daily newspaper.

JUST FOR KICKS, the headline read. Lisa, appropriately, was the featured player, with a color photo of her stretching for a ball stripped across the top of the page. Below was a large shot of Dana DiMuro and Cathy Wright scrambling for the ball while trying to avoid stepping on a fallen Clare Moore. To the right there was a snapshot of Ellen Paretti being carried off the field by Cathy Wright and Ginger Steuart after spraining her ankle.

While they all were smiling into the camera, Ellen wound up on crutches, out of action for weeks, hobbling after her kids and wondering if Andy, her husband, was going to get fed up with her new hobby (he didn't).

On and on it went, with the Madison Square Garden Network and Sports Channel New York taking the trail to Montclair and playing to simplistic and preconceived notions. Soccer moms weren't people with portfolios, with full and interesting lives. They were, well, soccer moms.

"Women a little too obsessed with their kids and who have nothing better to do," said Beth Fuqua, who had suspended her teaching career to raise two boys, Jeffrey and Griffin. Her husband, Howard Kerbel, often traveled for work, and they had decided that one parent should be home. There were financial sacrifices, though, and times when Beth missed the gratification of work.

Ginger Steuart, a certified public accountant, said she was secure enough not to care about societal labels. But Lisa found them "offensive, making us seem as if we did nothing before we had kids." These were issues, admittedly, that could not be easily explored in ninety-second spots, but the reality of this sudden and rather startling exposure was that the Montclair moms were cast as one-dimensional cutouts. None of them could be blamed for wondering why they had to be herded into some giant social holding pen.

Were fathers not at the wheels of the station wagons and on the sidelines every weekend, too? Weren't they generally even more obsessed with how their sons and daughters fared on the athletic fields? Why, then, were there no broad characterizations for them? Why weren't "soccer dads" a political target group? Given a similar set of circumstances—a half-dozen or more media reports on what men were doing in their spare time—it would be inconceivable that not one would have been asked what he did for a living.

It was true that Nina Sloan picked up her son from school, but that was when she was not rushing into Manhattan or some other location to produce or direct a television commercial. As a freelancer in a cutthroat industry, she had worked with, among others, the acknowledged king of global endorsement, Michael Jordan himself.

Nina, forty-one, grew up in Lynbrook, on Long Island, athletic and left out. "I tried out every year for cheerleading, and I never made it," she said. "I was crushed. If you didn't make cheerleading, you didn't have anything to do with sports. I was always a jock who didn't have an outlet. I was fast as a kid, faster than the boys in my grade. I also grew up in a family of very athletic people, particularly my mother, and she set the tone in the family for people playing sports. I danced from the time I was four, through high school. Had there been sports available, I would have jumped in. I come from a family where, typically, if something didn't exist, we would create it."

After she began playing soccer she just had to ask her mother, Helen, the chairman of the Department of Health and Nutrition Sciences at Brooklyn College, "What happened? Why weren't there sports for me?" No one really knew what to say other than to go for it now. Her life was already hectic, though. The only reason she even knew about the Wednesday morning group was that her sitter, a Montclair State University student, had been dating one of the trainers from Ashley's Soccer Camp, and had handed her a copy of the *New York Times* story.

Nina went once and was immediately hooked. "It really made me feel alive," she said. "Women always say their lives do not belong to them. But I'm out there and I'm not thinking that I have forty million things to do."

Mary Sibley was doing some scrambling herself, as the mother of two children, five and three years old, working as a health care consultant and teaching night courses at New York University. In the coming months her life would become even more demanding: She would volunteer to work for Bill Bradley and ultimately help write and present the health care proposal he used to launch his unsuccessful campaign for the Democratic presidential nomination. By the time Bradley conceded after Al Gore's Super Tuesday rout, Mary had appeared in a television commercial, written papers for his debate briefing book, represented the campaign before medical constituencies, ferried around visiting dignitaries, and leafleted in various locations, from the streets of suburban towns in the east to a cable car on the San Francisco hills. All while trying, and not always succeeding, not to miss a beat back home.

To Mary, forty-one, the notion of being labeled a soccer mom at this point in her life was downright hilarious. Though she had lettered in track for four years in high school in New Brunswick, New Jersey, Mary wasn't kidding herself; in a few short weeks she could tell she wasn't going to be giving up her day or night jobs. She wasn't Lisa, who was obviously picking up the skills as if they had been waiting for her out in the mailbox.

Mary had shown up only because Meg invited her following one of their aerobics classes. Mary found herself invigorated by the crispness of the weather, energized by the workout. "I realized it was very in-the-moment, nonintellectual," she said. "In a way, playing a sport like this changes your whole life identity. Most of us have no idea what the others do. There's no division, no class system. The size of your house doesn't matter. We don't talk about our professional sides."

Still, those other sides were part of who they were, even if the *Star-Ledger* and the friendly television people didn't ask. Cathy Wright, longtime marathoner and brand-new soccer-playing mom, was also Catherine LeCleire, a commercially successful print artist, college instructor, and lecturer. When she wasn't doing any of that, she could often be found at the Bradford School, which her two children attended, designing a mural or just painting a bench.

Diane Gray, mother of three, had made her professional mark in advertising at *The New York Times*. Beth Albert was the school's PTA copresident and a corporate public relations consultant for ESPN. Dana DiMuro, an art director, had been designing catalogs for fourteen years, supervising photo shoots and production. Barbara Martoglio had been a social worker and a tireless advocate for the elderly in northern New Jersey. Meg Goor, soon to be Hammond, was taking an active role in helping Ashley expand the burgeoning business of Montclair soccer.

And, of course, they all had to rouse their kids on school mornings, zip up the winter jackets, and pore over those homework sheets. They were school and community volunteers, and some had personal torches to carry. Laura Crandall, a trained physical therapist, was a stay-at-home mother, but she and her husband, Josh, feverishly lobbied New Jersey politicians to pass a law during the summer of 2000 establishing protocols for sudden unexplained death in childhood. In 1997 the Crandalls had lost their fifteen-month-old, Maria, to the murky affliction known as SIDS.

These women weren't necessarily filling time with soccer. The better question for many would have been, How do you find time?

And for those who were not active in the workforce, schools, or community, soccer may have been the first step back after a long run of changing diapers and making sure toddlers stayed off the stairs.

Sooner or later the kids began growing up, doing things for themselves. The time had to come for one's life to be reclaimed, and it wasn't just for kicks.

THE ONSET OF WINTER, bringing windchills that dropped the temperature near freezing, did not chase the women out of Brookdale Park. Nor did the Christmas vacation, with the children home from school, compel them to take a week off. They decided to hold the regular Wednesday session, and someone came up with the idea of soccer day care. This late December practice was the first time they played on family time. All of their soccer classes so far had been during the day, when the kids were at school, when the time was their own.

So the kids were at one end of the park, stepping through drills with a couple of Ashley's trainers, while their mothers scrimmaged away at the other end, their handbags and coffee thermoses marking the sidelines. When they ran through the drills, calling out to each other as they had been coached to do, their exhalations hovered like pallid puffs of smoke in the frosty morning air.

Most of the kids were played out after about an hour; the wind seemed to be swirling in their faces no matter which way they turned. It was, to be honest, not much of a day for soccer, or any other extended activity outdoors. Yet at the far end of the field it may as well have been sunny and pleasant: The women had paid for ninety minutes, and they were determined to use every one.

"Those first few months out in the park were joyous," Lisa said. "There was a passion you could feel. You looked around at all these women who had never had a chance to do this, and now we were doing it together. There was an absolute giddiness about being there."

They were developing staying power, outlasting even their normally inexhaustible children. Slowly, one after another, the little ones wandered across the park, their cheeks reddened and their bodies tired. They were making their case for a hasty retreat into warm cars. Their mothers waved at them, asking for a few more minutes, just a few more, pretty please. By the conclusion of the morning a remarkable role reversal had occurred. The children, resigned to their station, were on the sideline, watching, shouting encouragement, cheering for goals. The women had made their statement.

"We're going to play, and this is the way it's going to be," Lisa said. It was time for those in their lives to get used to it. It was, as well, time to get out of the cold and into the fire.

4

Choosing Up Sides

.

I<small>T WASN'T A DREAM</small>. It couldn't have been. Lisa knew this because her back was aching, a dull throb that made her climb out of bed gingerly and stand up straight. Stiff back and all, she felt as if she could have floated down the stairs. If a little back pain was the price of what she'd experienced the previous night, then so be it. She would happily pay.

The satisfaction of scoring two goals had been only part of it, and it wasn't even the most gratifying part. Lisa had been pumped up for this game, had sensed something in the air, and she had been right.

The indoor facility they were playing in was still under construction, with sawdust all over the lobby, and nature's call required a run to the Porta-Potti out in the chilly night air. But there was an artificial turf field, team benches, and a referee with a whistle and a stopwatch. The place had been electric, with so many of the kids and even some of the husbands around, with all the noise and tension of a game Lisa never expected to win.

Her team had overcome adversity and triumphed over injury, not to mention the opposition, in their dark blue shirts and shorts. Badgers, the opponents called themselves, and Lisa thought the name fit them like a goalie glove. "They had that attitude, cocky, hot shit, and I felt like, Who do they think they are?" she said. "This all started out friendly, playing hard and feeling good about your game. But with them, there was more anger than passion, something that just didn't sit right. They played too hard, too physical, too foul-mouthed. I didn't appreciate that, didn't see how it was warranted."

But she also saw that the Badgers, the outsiders, had raised the stakes. They had helped unleash an energy that was previously untapped in her, in everyone. A fierce rivalry had instantly heated up and detonated on the field.

Lisa had come home after a victory drink at Tierney's Tavern, the old smoke-filled townie hangout, the kind of bar where you could drink your life's first beer and your last. She couldn't calm down, couldn't get to sleep. She couldn't let go. Hours later, Lisa still felt like waking up the world and crying out a thousand sports clichés. Her team, the newly formed Bluestone Belles, had shown character and resolve. She and her new friends had won the war, although she did have to admit that the Belles had left the field with significant casualties as well.

"I'm scared—I don't want to do this," Clare Moore had yelled out in her Scottish accent when the ref had told them to form a wall, to protect the goal. Anna Girdwood, the Englishwoman who coached girls' teams for Ashley and had presumably played soccer for most of her life, was lining up her free kick from a few feet away.

"Don't worry about it, you'll be OK," Dana DiMuro assured Clare.

Whack! Clare took a rifle shot, right in the chest, the ball drawn to her as if it were targeting fear itself. She hadn't been able to use her arms reflexively to protect herself because they were held by teammates who had tried to calm her down. Clare spent most of the game on the sideline, doubled over, a pale-faced reminder that soccer is a contact sport.

Her two children, seven and five, sat stone-faced waiting for a sign that Mommy was all right. She wasn't, at least not right enough to play any more that evening.

Lisa and the rest of the Belles all wondered why Anna had to try to drive the ball through the wall like that. What in the world had she been trying to prove? The pace and fury of the game seemed to invite injuries. Even before taking the ball in the chest, Clare was scratched on her arm with a ring, despite rules that clearly called for no jewelry to be worn on the field.

"When you come across a team like that, it just raises your game," Lisa said. "Personally, I come up against someone overly competitive, I'll go the extra. I just come right back with it." Lisa found herself pushing on as she had never done before. She could almost hear the creaking of her vertebrae on throw-ins, and when she really got her foot into the ball, she felt the occasional throb. It wasn't all that different from what she felt from general stress, though. She convinced herself it was no big deal.

Ginger Steuart, by contrast, knew she was taking a risk playing this game, or any game. The surgeon who had fixed her knee after the skiing accident had seen his share of wrecked ligaments as the orthopedist for the Oakland Raiders football team. "Don't plan on becoming a professional athlete," he'd told her.

This game was as close as she got, and would ever get. Sure enough, her knee buckled, and Ginger cried out in pain, hobbled off, headed back to the medical center.

Now Lisa's team was down to one substitute against an outfit that had serious soccer players, young players, including an aggressive little hothead named Ravan who was all over the field, slamming into people, screaming at the heavens and even her teammates. "Oh, great, nice time to fix your hair!" she had mocked a fellow Badger, a soccer mom, when the poor woman had paused on a throw-in to brush the hair from her eyes.

Lisa and Co. didn't know quite what to make of this, and, really, how could they? One week they were all in the park, sharing politically correct, up-with-us encounters of the athletic kind. Now they found themselves in the middle of a trash talk convention. It wasn't the time, however, to debate the pros and cons of this accelerated track, not with elbows planted in their backs and bodies flying and most of them being forced to find a competitive edge they didn't know they had.

But the Belles met the enemy, and they didn't back down. Lisa scored. One of her new teammates, a forty-four-year-old cyclone named Jeanne Jeffrey, scored two more. Anna scored all three for the Badgers. The game had seesawed, 1–0 for the Belles, then 1–1; 2–1 for them, then 2–2; 3–2 for them, then 3–3. The noise inside the brand-new soccer dome was deafening. The kids were cheering. The husbands were offering advice, much of it unwanted. The time left in the game was dwindling. Finally, Lisa's hard shot off the right foot from point-blank range found the back of the net, a game winner that would represent so much to them in the coming weeks and beyond.

"I didn't even know we won," Lisa would say. "When we finished, I actually thought we'd tied. It was a crazy game, a really good game. We were working so hard. I loved it so much. Jeanne and I— we felt unstoppable. I lost count of the score, but I kept on going. I wanted to go and go and go."

Poof. She woke up the next morning. Had it all been a dream? Whoa. Her aching back—and that, come to think of it, wasn't all that hurt—reminded her it most certainly was not.

They had gone out afterward, ignoring the fact that they all had to be up early the next morning, as they did every morning. They decided to worry about that later.

"Now you understand better why I need to go out with the guys after we play hockey," Brain had said to her. You want to share the experience, retell and replay it, savor it, and have a few laughs.

Dana, the team comedian, made everyone crack up when she said she'd spent half the game shooting dirty looks at her husband, Declan, for his constant yelling of instructions. Everyone seemed to have lost it a little bit, especially Dana, when she'd flipped Anna the bird. Dana had been awarded an indirect penalty kick outside the box, and Anna was screaming at her less-inclined teammates to form the wall. Dana found it all very amusing, as if she, a novice, was going to drive the ball as powerfully as Anna had earlier. "And as if," Dana said, "I was actually going to make the shot."

She caught Anna's eye. Unaccountably, her middle finger shot straight up in the air.

"I can't believe you did that," Anna told her when the game ended, taking it for the joke that it was. "You could have been red-carded."

"Red-carded," Dana said. "What's that?"

THE FINGER, then the arm. The toe, then the leg. It was all a new experience, move by move, play by play, game by game, everyone into the water, and the deep end at that. Swimming or soccer, what was the difference if you didn't know the strokes?

Ready or not, a maternal blow for athletic Darwinism had been struck in Montclair. Several weeks before Lisa's dream game would so dramatically come true, almost four months after the first ball was kicked, she had again taken the initiative for the soccer-playing moms' next evolutionary step.

But it hadn't dawned on Rochelle Sandler, at least not right away, what Lisa and Ginger had been up to watching from the sideline one Wednesday morning, studying the rest of them as if they were laboratory mice dribbling about a maze. *Calculating,* is the word Rochelle had settled on, but the more appropriate term, as applied to the formation of a sports team, was *scouting.* Lisa and Ginger had taken it upon themselves to choose up sides.

Soccer Domain, the new indoor facility, was about to open for business in Depot Square, along the railroad tracks near the center of town. Steven Plofker—Bobbi Brown's husband and a local lawyer and real estate developer—was the financier behind the so-called dome. Plofker, whose office was right across the street, had struck an operational deal with—who else?—Ashley Hammond.

It was fortuitous timing on Ashley's part. The media attention had accelerated the growth of the women's clinics, outdoor and indoor, which meant he now had more than enough players to begin a league and to help get his latest venture off to a rousing start. The dome was fitted with a durable synthetic rubberized grass field, not quite full-sized, but big enough to comfortably accommodate a game with seven players a side, goalie included. Now all the women had to do was determine how those sides were going to be cast.

"When I heard that they were forming teams and everyone was saying, 'Oh, I'm going to be playing inside,'" Rochelle said, "I said, 'I'll send in the application, too.'" She made the mistake of assuming that the regulars from the Wednesday morning group would form their own entry. But that group had grown well beyond the size of one team. The first hard-knocks lesson of team sports was about to be learned: When the opening round of phone calls were made and Rochelle didn't get one, she realized she hadn't made the cut.

She felt like a kid left sitting on the side. "I had been part of that original group, and I thought of these women as new friends," she said. "I was already feeling vulnerable at the time, having lost my father. I found this very discouraging."

She felt that Lisa and Ginger were asking only the best players to join them, but that sentiment wasn't entirely fair. Ellen Paretti, Beth Albert, and Barbara Martoglio were all flattered to be asked to join the team, but they worried that they were not good enough to meet whatever the standard was going to be.

If Lisa and Ginger were guilty of anything, it was seizing the moment, setting the ground rules. The truth was that someone had to take the first step, though to Rochelle and several of the others it seemed overly aggressive, somewhat insensitive to the group-hug sensibilities of those who had crossed the sideline together. Many of the women just assumed that Steve Cook, David Law, and Ashley would assign them to teams. It would be balanced that way. It would be fair. Wasn't that how it worked with the kids?

But Ashley didn't see it that way. These weren't children. The women, he said, needed to be given "ownership" of their league. They needed to accept the fact that, sooner or later, competition and the acknowledgment of skill level would enter the equation. If they were going to play a team sport and be serious about it, they might as well deal with this now.

For some, though, it was happening too fast. Susan Hatzopoulos had begun to understand that many of the women cared far more about excelling, about winning, than she did. She had been playing tennis for some time now, playing less to win than to improve, playing for the love of the game, the social activity, the simple joy of being outdoors. For her, that was what soccer had been, better only because it was bigger. She never relished the idea of playing indoors, of keeping score. During the outdoor scrimmages she began to "daydream," to emotionally retreat. Competitive soccer, she decided, was not for her.

But for every Susan going, there was a Venera Gashi and a Jeanne Jeffrey coming. There were women who had waited years for an opportunity just like this. And everyone could plainly see that Venera and Jeanne were, in the vernacular of team sports, first-round draft picks.

Venera grew up in a family from Kosovo, Serbia, that had settled in Brooklyn when she was four. Her brothers were all soccer players, and she had grown up playing right along with them, tall and skilled, until they went off to the parks for games with rough-and-tumble men, leaving their sister with no place to play. Venera was a young child when Title IX was passed. It was still too late for her, though, as the funding and implementation of athletic programs for girls in the Bensonhurst section of Brooklyn was slow to come around.

Years later, having settled in Montclair, Venera would drop off her son Jack at Ashley's Soccer Camp and realize that her appetite for the sport was beginning to return. She even had a passing thought of starting her own mothers' team. Then her husband, Matt, clipped the *New York Times* story about the Montclair soccer moms, and Venera read it aloud with glee. She got hold of Lisa's phone number. The following Wednesday couldn't come soon enough.

Jeanne Jeffrey lived in North Caldwell and taught kindergarten in Montclair. No one would have believed that she'd never played soccer, given the way Jeanne, so light on her feet, threw her body around the gymnasium. With Jeanne's shock of whitish blond hair, Lisa couldn't miss her when she checked out the night clinic scene one night. Soccer, it turned out, was about the only sport Jeanne was a stranger to. A tomboy tagalong to five athletic brothers on the fields of Maplewood, New Jersey, she was one of her generation's exceptions, to whom sports became a lifelong habit, a family staple. Her three daughters played sports. She, in fact, had met her husband playing a killer game, rugby, years ago in Montclair.

Lisa had nine players now, a ready-made roster. And as long as she had taken it this far, she went out and got herself a sponsor, too. The Bluestone Café on Watchung Avenue agreed to supply uniform shirts. Lisa and Ginger decided to call their new team the Bluestone Belles. It had a nice ring. Now it was up to the others, however reluctantly, to follow their lead.

"I never would have thought to organize a team," Beth Fuqua said. "But Lisa worked the phone. She said, 'Are you going to sign up?' I said, 'Well, I'll try it.' Then two weeks later Lisa called again and said, 'Will you be the contact person for your team?' I said I could make phone calls. Then I'm calling people I don't know and saying, 'Hi, you're on my soccer team. Our first game is . . .'

"Then it's the first game, and the referee says, 'OK, Captain, time for the coin toss.' All of a sudden I'm a captain. It made me laugh, 'cause I am the most noncaptain personality. And now people are saying, 'What should we do?' I said, 'Please, I just want to make this team list and make a few phone calls.'"

Beth's team ultimately came from the Wednesday group, mostly those who had not been chosen by Lisa: Beth Panucci and Nina Sloan, Rochelle Sandler and Diane Gray, Mary Sibley, Sue O'Donnell and her younger sister, Laura Crandall, who had played some soccer in high school. Their best player was Camilla Bertelsen, a nineteen-year-old au pair from Denmark who had read Lisa's flyer seeking "adult" women players at the Union Congregation nursery school.

She called Lisa, assuming *adult* meant women in their midtwenties. She had never known any "real adult" women who played. Her own roster set, Lisa steered Camilla to Beth Fuqua.

"I was shocked," Camilla said upon meeting her new teammates, the Pokémoms. Camilla didn't quite get the team name. Since she wasn't ten years old, why would she? The Pokémon hysteria was just taking root in the States and in Cathy Wright's house with her two children. Cathy got the idea for the team name, and then for the matching shirts, with POKÉMOMS across the front and with a modification of the motto —"Gotta kick 'em all"—scripted on the back.

"What is a Poké?" Rochelle had asked. "Do we want to be slow?" By the following week her own boys had enlightened her. "Cool name," she thought.

Beth's team was out of the starting gate, albeit at a slightly different pace than Lisa's. The Pokémoms were part of the more laid-back pack, along with the Beanie Babes, the Hot Flashes, the Chicks with Cleats, and the Pride. A team from a nearby town was going by the menacing name of the Livingston Soccer Moms.

The choice of names was all in the spirit of fun, another way of creating a mandate that this not be taken too seriously too soon.

"But you could already see that the Pokémom culture was very different than, for instance, the Bluestone Belles'," Mary Sibley said. "They were athletic, and they had those uniform shirts, and they really looked like they knew what they were doing. Most of us literally did not know how to do a throw-in."

The last thing Mary wanted from soccer, from this game she had called "nonintellectual," was the pressure to excel. An adventurous type, Mary had even volunteered to play goal, and fared reasonably well in the first game. So had the team, losing to the Bluestone Belles by only 4–2. That had been surprising, encouraging; they hadn't expected to beat Lisa's team, or even come close. The Belles had played aggressively but not threateningly. Opening night at the Soccer Domain had actually been a hoot.

Then came week two. The Pokémoms stepped onto the field against the Badgers, who were outfitted in navy blue Italian-made Kappa jerseys and matching shorts. They had young, aggressive players. They had tall, athletic moms.

The game, and the onslaught, began. "They were the coaches and the coaches' girlfriends," Mary said. "We were practically in shock."

With shots coming at her from all directions, the score mounting as in a pinball game, Mary felt like the duck in a shooting gallery, fortunate to get off the field before she needed to rewrite her own health care policy, much less Bill Bradley's.

Meanwhile Lisa's team, slotted for the next game, had come in early and got a firsthand look at the serious competition. With the exception of Ashley's wife, Meg, they didn't recognize any of these Badgers. They weren't among the original soccer moms, or even those who had later come to play in the park. From the sideline some of them looked awfully young. They looked like ringers.

When some of the Badgers stayed around afterward to watch the next game, the Belles felt as if they were being sized up, being challenged to show them what they could do. So they did. Changing character from the previous week, the Belles proceeded to annihilate the outclassed Hot Flashes, 9–0.

It didn't take much of a sports enthusiast to see that a challenge had been made, and battle lines drawn. Next up for the Belles were the big, bad Badgers; at stake, bragging rights in a league that was all of two weeks old. Athletic egos seemed to be asserting themselves after having been locked away in storage for years. This had all happened so fast, but Lisa had to admit that her competitive spirit was surging, and she went home that week and did what a true captain must do when the call for leadership comes. She found a new goalie, hired a coach, and summoned her team to the practice field.

I F ONLY they had been there, Meg thought. If only Lisa and those snooty Bluestone Belles could have seen us at our very first practice just a few weeks ago. Practice? Yeah, right. It was more like a getting-acquainted session.

"Ball, come over here and say hello to foot."

"Foot, meet ball."

The Belles' players, park regulars for months, would have had themselves a hearty laugh, like Tony Meola did.

"Look at what my career has come to," Tony had said that day, quite a way for an American World Cup star to be celebrating his thirtieth birthday.

Big deal, Meg said; so the Badgers had the longtime goalie for the U.S. men's national team and former MetroStar show them a few fundamentals and basic formations. Tony and his wife, Colleen, had recently settled in Montclair with their young son. Colleen, tall, fair, and slender, looked like the prototypical athlete, and she had to know a lot more about this game than the average soccer-playing mom.

Appearances can be deceiving, though. Colleen Meola hadn't seriously kicked a ball in fifteen years, when she quit playing soccer to become a cheerleader at Kearny High.

Most of the Badgers, in fact, were West Orange mothers, complete novices, bumping into each other, exasperating themselves one moment and breaking up laughing the next. As far as Meg was concerned, the core Badgers were more a coffee klatch or family circle than a sports team.

Laura Barker, who was dating one of the guys who worked with Ashley, had told her cousin, Amy Roy, about the soccer moms over in Montclair; Amy, mother of four and a professional photographer, had called Meg, an old friend, who had not been invited to join any of the teams.

"We'll make our own," Amy said.

Amy called around, starting with her sister, Minnie Evans, and then Kelly Corbett and her sister, Linda Davis. Holly Silver said she would check with her sister, Colleen Meola, and their cousin, Noreen. Karen Aronson, another friend, said she'd give it a try.

"I thought we'd be at the bottom," Meg said. "I had no idea we'd be any good."

But it turned out Minnie, Karen, and Noreen picked up the

game pretty fast. Meg played in goal the first couple of games, and wasn't bad at all, even if she felt overmatched the first few times anyone made a run at her with the ball.

Mainly thanks to Anna and Ravan, the first two games were pretty one-sided, and Meg didn't have too much to worry about. They took it easy on the nice women from Livingston, who apparently hadn't realized that not everyone was a complete beginner when she signed on. It wasn't until the Pokémoms, with those cute shirts, and, granted, that game was pretty lopsided, 8–1, that Meg and the others said, Enough, let's back off.

The next thing they knew, people were staring at the Badgers from the sideline as if they had been beamed in from the planet Amazon. "Like we were some superteam, a bunch of professionals," Meg said.

The truth, she said, was that she had never seen Anna Girdwood, or Ravan Magrath, for that matter, play. It wasn't as if she had gone out and recruited either of them for the purpose of winning a trophy. Well, all right, in Anna's case she figured it wouldn't hurt to have a soccer coach on the team, someone who knew what she was doing. Anna had been living with Meg and Ashley and the kids, and Meg had told her, "Play for us or I'm not cooking for you." Anna was twenty-four years old, a stranger in town, in the country, and what Meg really wanted was for her to get out of the house, to meet some people.

As for Ravan, she came via the Steve Plofker–Bobbi Brown connection. Ravan was the day sitter for Bobbi's three boys, and Bobbi called Amy, asking if she knew of a team Ravan might play for. Not knowing the women on the other teams, Amy took it upon herself to volunteer her own.

She hadn't bothered to ask Bobbi for a scouting report, or for game films of Ravan in action at Bloomfield High or at the state college up in Ramapo, where she'd been the goalie as a freshman. All

Amy or any of them knew was that Ravan was twenty, she had dropped out of college, she was in the throes of a family crisis, and Bobbi and Steve had practically adopted her.

Ravan's mother, Cindy, was dying of breast cancer. "Soccer is my life," she liked to say, and at this point it was somewhere she could just let loose.

Of course the Badgers were appalled by Ravan's on-field behavior, especially since at least half of it was directed at them. The older women on the team appealed to her to calm down. They lectured her. They coddled her. They yelled at her.

"I know I was obscene that game, and I apologized to my teammates," she would say. "I was screaming at everybody. I was out of control. I know I need to control myself." She was always remorseful and sincere, pulling her baseball cap so low you almost couldn't see her eyes.

What were the Badgers supposed to do? Pull all the other players aside and say, "Her mother's dying, give her a break, OK?" For women who had not been raised to compete physically at any skill level, who were out on that field on a whim and a prayer, Ravan was the polar opposite of OK. She was a temperamental, intimidating nightmare.

Meg and the Badgers understood the visceral reaction; what they couldn't figure out was why they were considered guilty by association. Why grown women, mothers and professionals, had formed teams that also seemed to be behaving like high school cliques. They didn't understand why, as Meg said, "women you were playing soccer with twice a week would walk right past you and not say hello." She didn't know what to make of Lisa and her team, the Belles. "We're over here and they're over there and no one says anything to anyone."

From where the Badgers stood, it was the Belles who were taking all of this much too seriously. They hadn't exactly taken pity on the

Hot Flashes, now had they? And weren't they the ones who had called a Sunday morning practice and strategy session before the game against the Badgers? Pumped the Pokémoms for tips on how to play them? Hired Karen Sherris—actually paying her per practice session—to come down and coach?

The new Belles goalie, the blonde with the ponytail who must have made a half-dozen diving saves, who threw her body around the turf like some teenage gymnast, Meg would've bet she couldn't have been a day over twenty-five. The word the Badgers had on Sarah Hogan, a nanny, was that she was a former high school and state select team player out on the West Coast. Meg and her team wondered how Sarah fit into a collection of soccer-playing moms any more than Anna or Ravan.

Then there was the tall one, Venera, who stayed back on defense. She had such long legs, you couldn't get around her without the ball, much less with it. The older one, Jeanne—the one Ravan took it easy on because one of Bobbi's kids had had her for kindergarten? "Mrs. Jeffrey," as Ravan called her, didn't exactly need to be pitied, the way she dished out the elbows. Plus she was fast, just like Lisa, who was relentless and could unleash a shot off either foot.

Let's be honest, Meg thought; Ravan was a defensive player, but half the time she was so emotional, so out of control. If not for Anna, the Belles would have shut the Badgers out. What then, besides Ravan, made the Badgers so different from the Belles?

Anna said she couldn't understand what the fuss, the tension, was about. It occurred to her that something was askew when she had Beth Albert's five-year-old, Charlie, in a youth clinic and, kidding around, called him a "little Badger." "I'm not a Badger," he said. "They stink."

Couldn't these teams coexist? Wasn't it better to have a close game, a 4–3 game, than to win 9–0 or 8–1? For her money Anna said she was "energized, overjoyed," just to have played in such a competitive match. Everyone should have gone out together, Anna said, to the pub and raised a glass to a job well done.

But while the Belles celebrated at Tierney's, the Badgers retreated to their own hangout, at a bar they called the Hat, across the border, in West Orange.

Two bitter rivals had done battle, gritted their teeth, shook hands, nodded grimly, and gone their own ways. It was very European, very clannish, as Ashley knew all too well.

5

Belles of the Ball

D ON'T BE AFRAID to get the ball, to make a mistake,"
Camilla would tell Beth Fuqua, captain of the Pokémoms,
a woman twice her age. "It's OK—you don't have to pass
to me," Beth would say.

"But, Beth," Camilla would say, "how else are you going to learn?"

Camilla Bertelsen had come to the United States to learn,
observe, and absorb. She had come to work on her English, already
startlingly proficient, and to take in as much of the country and culture as she could in one year. With the wide-eyed exuberance of a
nineteen-year-old adventurer from a Danish countryside town of six
hundred, she had come to play—but never dreamed that her play-
mates would be women truly old enough to have been her mother.

"What am I doing with these older women?" she asked herself in
the beginning.

But before long she was calling home, collect call for Mom, from Pokémom.

"Wouldn't it be fun to have a team like this one at home?" Camilla asked Lilly Bertelsen. The thought was laughed away. Camilla knew that her mother would never play on a team with her, or with anyone else. She had to admit that before meeting these Montclair mothers, she found the thought of a woman past her thirty-fifth birthday playing soccer completely absurd. Yet now Camilla was struck by the realization that her mother, at forty-four, was younger than some of her teammates.

Perhaps she just couldn't imagine her mother acting like a kid, in the way most children cannot imagine their parents having sex. No, Camilla said, there was something about these women in Montclair, something energizing and different. "Maybe it's because they are playing a sport, but they don't look like older women," she said. "They look younger."

It wasn't as if every woman Camilla had met here impressed her as dynamic, or happy. Others she had come across seemed bored, preoccupied with material things. Camilla's father worked in construction, and her mother cleaned houses; they certainly weren't well off by the standards she was exposed to in Montclair. Some of the women she had met dropping off and picking up the children at school or idling away the autumn afternoons in the park had everything—spacious homes, designer clothes, fancy cars. Yet a few didn't seem to be doing anything with their free time except devising more ways to spend their husbands' money. One woman she knew had no job but employed a full-time nanny and was in her pajamas every morning until eleven. "I have a really good picture of what I don't want to become," Camilla said.

She had been in Montclair only a few months but was already aware of the disparity of wealth, and the numbing pursuit of it. This, for her, was no shining example of America the beautiful. The infatuation with stock prices and house values in the most casual conversations made her wistful for down-home values, but her perceptions of town and country began to soften when she met Lisa. This was someone who had that big house and all the trimmings but was heavily invested in soccer, in people, as something for herself, her friends, and even a teenager she had only just met.

"She called me up and said, 'We're having soccer on Wednesday morning—why don't you come?'" Camilla said. "Then we go out for coffee—Lisa, Clare, Dana, and some of the other Belles. It was chat, chat, them wanting to know all about me, my home, my family. I'm sitting with them, and every once in a while I think, They're twenty years older than I am."

They had taken an immediate and perhaps inevitable liking to Camilla, whose appearance screamed Scandinavia, with her short, dark blond hair, her round, light eyes, and a smile that helped illuminate the dome. To the older women she was the anti-Ravan, engaging and unthreatening. She had played soccer since the age of seven, but on the field with the Pokémoms it was obvious she had nothing to prove.

"In the beginning, I almost didn't want to show what I could do," Camilla said. "It's so hard to learn a sport at forty. I didn't want to ruin it for them, I guess. When I went for the ball, I wouldn't use my shoulder or hips." Except for the game against the Badgers, against Ravan. In that game the competitive Camilla emerged, hips and forearms in motion, "getting away with whatever the ref doesn't see." This was the way she played back home, the way the game was supposed to be played. "At home, Ravan would not have been a problem," Camilla said, referring to the physical style of play.

She had no personal problem with Ravan; Camilla had played against emotional girls her whole life. One day she struck up a conversation with Ravan while dropping off one of the girls she took care of at the Watchung Elementary School. Ravan had a young boy,

Bobbi Brown's oldest, in tow; she was open and friendly, much different than she was in cleats.

"Nice person," Camilla decided. She understood why it was so much easier for her to bridge the gap than it was for the older women. As a young athlete she recognized the need to leave certain attitudes on the field. If she'd carried home every slight, every wound, she would have had no friends—at least none from soccer.

Lisa, Meg, and the rest of the Belles and Badgers would figure this out, Camilla guessed. She already was amazed at how much they had learned about the game, how quickly they were picking up the moves and the mood—the Belles especially. They were more aggressive than the Pokémoms, surer of themselves, with a greater sense of entitlement. At the dome, in the bar, they reminded Camilla of some of the teams she had played on back home.

To an impressionable, hopeful, and watchful teenager, all these older women were fascinating, inspirational. Camilla could not believe Cathy Wright's runner's stamina. Nina Sloan—who had become the Pokémom goalie—turned out to be a natural at the position, with the athletic instincts to match her nimble dancer's feet. The two Beths, Fuqua and Panucci, were getting better every time they played, even if they were still apologizing for every misstep and mistake. She found herself becoming more comfortable with being their mentor, even their cheerleader.

"We need a win," she would goad them on the sideline. "We're going to get a win."

"OK, Camilla," they would tell her, giggling like, well, nineteen-year-olds. "If you say so."

She looked forward to going out to Tierney's with Lisa and Co. on Wednesday nights. She would sip her beer, munch on onion rings; just your average bunch of mothers in handsome soccer jerseys and a nineteen-year-old in a Pokémoms shirt. She was tickled by the irony, and could already picture the shirt on the wall above her bed back home in Denmark. She would never forget these wonderful nights, this adult education, a peek into what could be and what she hoped would be her future.

She would listen intently to these women, with their tales of juggling work and children, and their complaints about the ungodly hours their husbands were working and all for—what? It was no wonder that they all seemed so much younger to Camilla than their birth certificates would suggest. During those times in the park, and under the dome, and in the bar, the mothers were on Camilla's more idealistic territory, believing that life had to be more than a four-bedroom Colonial and financial security. They made her understand why she had decided to experience America in the first place. She had come not only for fun and games, for enlightenment and empowerment, but also to discover that no matter how large and frightening the world might be, there was always a support group, a team, a friend. There was always someone, somewhere, to count on.

I T WASN'T LONG AFTER the Badgers–Belles conflict that Venera Gashi felt the tragedy of real war. She picked up the telephone one day in her Glen Ridge home and heard the urgency and pain in the voice of her father-in-law, just minutes away in Montclair. Her in-laws, by a quirk of fate, were visiting in the States when the war in Kosovo broke out. Now Venera's father-in-law was saying that her forty-six-year-old brother-in-law, Ajet, had been forced to flee his Kosovo home with his wife and four children. At least they hoped that the family had escaped the Serbs, and made it out of their small village alive.

Sheremet (Americanized to Matt), Gashi's older brother, lived in a hotbed of rebel activity, and his village was therefore one of the first to come under Serbian attack. The thought of Slobodan Milosevic's henchmen coming across her sixteen-year-old niece was enough to send a chill down Venera's spine. And who knew what fate Ajet had met? Matt was keeping a stiff upper lip because he had to, if only for the sake of his parents and his own children. Already, though, the reports and rumors were flooding the Internet: The Albanian men who didn't escape into the mountains were being murdered and tossed into mass graves.

To Venera, this was no abstract conflict on a faraway continent. This was a horror that hit home and hit hard. The Gashis were a close family; Venera, Matt, and the children had spent entire summers with Ajet and his family in Kosovo. Venera could visualize where the children played and slept. Now they were all on the run, statistics in a brutal ethnic cleansing. "For me, there were uncles and aunts and all my cousins, too," she said. "I have to say, it was the worst personal experience of my life."

She was a true child of the Balkans, born to a Croatian mother and an Albanian father. Her family left the region and settled in Brooklyn, but in the tradition of first-generation immigrants, they maintained close ties to their homeland. Her brothers played regular soccer games with other Albanians in Brooklyn's Marine Park. She married Matt, who had attended medical school at the University of Kosovo and was doing his residency training in the States. Unlike her husband, Venera had grown up with American culture, but she never lost touch with her roots. "We had a house in Kosovo," she said. It hadn't been long into the war that their house, like so many others, was leveled.

The Serbian invasion was a nightmarish intrusion on what had been "a wonderful time." After so many years Venera had rediscovered soccer, an experience that revitalized her and forced her into the best shape of her childbearing years. Her children were involved, wanting to go to the dome to watch Mom play. Her parents and one of her brothers had recently moved to Montclair and dropped in from time to time to form their own little Bluestone Belles rooting section. "It kind of lifted my self-esteem. coming from Pampers and all that," Venera said. "We were getting into a sport that more and more women were identifying with as something of our own. You felt good about yourself. It was something just for you."

When only a weather event of biblical proportion could stop them from playing outdoors, Matt had watched her strap on her shin guards one particularly frigid morning. "What are you doing?" he said.

The answer was complex, emotional. This was about more than a game. It was about everything that came along with it. "Coffee, drinks, a wonderful workout," Venera said. "For me, exercise had to be some kind of play, something social. It wasn't like I'd gained a lot of weight, but I wasn't in good shape. The first few times, I couldn't breathe, but then I began to run the whole time without any problems at all. I'm thirty-four, and I'd look at someone like Jeanne, about ten years older than I am, and she was an inspiration for me."

Now Venera had to ask herself how she could continue to play while her husband, her family, and practically her entire heritage was in peril, on the verge of collapse. Already, just a handful of weeks after the war began, it was taking a toll on her daily life. Doing the chores around the house, paying the bills—it all began to feel meaningless, futile. When a friend complained that a whole floor of her house had caved in, Venera felt like shouting, "You think that's a problem?" Even her ability to stay on top of the children's schoolwork suffered. But as it turned out, beyond the daily Internet missions and the ongoing quest for news, the only routine she remained faithful to during those dark days was soccer.

"I made a decision that I was going to go no matter how bad things got at home," she said. "And believe me, it got very depressing at times."

Initially, her teammates would see her pull into the parking lot for Sunday practice, or push through the revolving doors from the lobby of the dome, and they'd wait for a private moment to ask: "Have you heard from Matt's brother?" After a while, Lisa said, they could see that having to repeat herself—"No, nothing yet, thank you for asking"—was only making Venera feel worse. What became apparent was that soccer was her escape. "We just let her know we were there for her," Lisa said.

"I'd go there and play, not with the joy that I was able to feel before," Venera said. "It was stress relief, and the women realized that it was a place I didn't want to deal with it. I just wanted to play, and forget.

"I know there were times that I was very angry about what I'd read in the newspaper, children being killed, and I would go out there and play very aggressively, almost in anger, and I'd do real well. I could see some of the women on the other team didn't know what to make of it."

In a sense, though she was fifteen years older and able to hide her emotions better, Venera was using soccer much the way Ravan Magrath was. Venera was an imposing defender, with her height and broad shoulders. Many of the women who were complete beginners were almost afraid to engage her.

Week after week she just played the game, went home, and waited for the word that came later in the spring that Ajet's wife and children had safely reached the Albanian border. They had been forced to leave their home by tractor, allowed to take only the clothes they wore.

Venera and Matt and their parents filled out documents to bring them to New Jersey, but it was mainly those refugees who had crossed into Macedonia that were being allowed to leave. Money was wired to Albania so Ajet's wife and children could temporarily house and feed themselves, so they could survive and safely await news of Ajet's fate.

As the weeks and the war dragged on, Venera could see it had affected her children—Jack, who was twelve, and Nicky, seven. The local newspaper in Glen Ridge had written about the family. The kids felt like celebrities for a day or two, but, unlike her teammates on the Belles, they didn't know when to stop seeking updates from her. "Did you hear anything yet?" they'd ask, hoping as much for a return to their own domestic normalcy as for a sign that their relatives were safe and sound.

Finally, after the shelling of Serbia had forced Milosevic to retreat and the peacekeeping forces entered Kosovo, the news arrived that Ajet was alive and had come out of the mountains. He was reunited with his family, and they returned to their home, to rebuild.

The dark cloud quickly disappeared from Venera's life, and when it did she felt strong, proud of herself for having had the resilience to cope in such a productive way. She was grateful that she had not given up soccer, had not missed out on the chance to build on the new friendships she'd made.

Even under normal circumstances, Venera considered herself more homebody than barfly. During the weeks of the war, it was only on the rarest of occasions that the Belles could coax her out to Tierney's for a drink. She would go on special occasions, such as a teammate's birthday. She had known these women only a short time, but she felt close to them, and she'd learned there was truth in the cliché that sports can bring people together quickly. Her teammates understood; they knew what she needed beyond their quiet care and support. She needed to play, to run, to feel the high of individual achievement within the group dynamic. She needed to hear them shout her name for a clean header, a well-timed pass, and that was all she needed, because execution required concentration and concentration meant relief and relief kept her going.

Soccer demanded that Venera keep going. "Soccer," she would say, "kept me sane."

. . .

THE NIGHT OF April 14th brought the last game of the first league season. Sarah Hogan couldn't make it, and the undefeated Belles had to play against Chicks with Cleats without their starting goalie, their only "young" player. Sarah's absence, however, would not be a problem; only the Badgers, it turned out, were their competitive equals in that first round of games.

Mothers all, the Belles lined up in front of the net for their championship team photo. They shared the feeling that this was the way it should be, the first league championship trophy going home with the woman who had started it. "Lisa and most of the women on this team were the ones who were out there all winter," Venera said.

Standing in the back row of the photo were Ginger, Venera, Jeanne, Beth Albert, and Clare. Front row: Lisa, Dana, Ellen, and Barbara Martoglio, who went home that night and placed the trophy on the entertainment center in her living room. When the photo was developed, she framed it and put it in front of the trophy. Her husband, Ed, called it the shrine.

"The picture is so much more important to me than the trophy," Barbara said. "I just really like that picture."

For her it was like being a kid again. She was one of the few mothers who had reaped the benefits of team sports, while growing up. It was difficult to believe now, but she had been a "sheltered, shy, chubby, and four-eyed girl" going from Catholic school to high school in Clifton, New Jersey. Her grades, she said, were "mediocre." Her confidence was low.

Several girls at the school were interested in track and were pushing for the chance to be on the same team with the boys. The boys' football coach decided to nip that insurrection in the bud by starting a track team for girls. Barbara made the team as a javelin thrower. "It was great, it was gratifying, and it brought me out of my shell," she said. "It really changed my personality."

She went out for field hockey and later became captain. As a senior she won a trophy for being the most accomplished female athlete in her school. She went off to college confident and extroverted, believing that having played team sports—not necessarily excelling, just participating—had "really helped shape the rest of my life."

Barbara and Ed Martoglio were known around Montclair as people with heart. They had four children, including an adopted African-American daughter, not much of an issue, if one at all, in racially diverse Montclair. Despite the demands of motherhood, Barbara had continued her social work, and her role as executive director for Senior Services. "I derive a lot of fulfillment from working, and just being home was never enough," she said. "I'd come to the conclusion that I really need to work—for me, for my marriage."

Ed Martoglio was a licensed attorney who several years before had come to his own realization that he needed more of an emotional return from his work than tax law could give him. He went into the business of buying and renovating residential properties to provide stable housing in the area for families in need.

One of the first properties Ed and his partner, Alfred Pierri, purchased and redeveloped was an apartment building in nearby Orange, New Jersey. One of the tenants in that building was DelFrances Bennett, a young single mother on welfare with two young girls. Ed became friendly with DelFrances, occasionally taking her girls out for ice cream. The following year, when an apartment became available in another of his properties—a house on North Fullerton Avenue in Montclair—Ed offered it to DelFrances. The children would be better off, he suggested, in Montclair's public schools.

DelFrances accepted the apartment, and the Martoglios took a special liking to the earnest woman they came to know as Del. When she had a third daughter with a different man from the father of her first two, the older girls stayed with Ed and Barbara. The children in the two families became close; as the years passed the Martoglios—who once had fretted about their ability to bear children—suddenly found themselves looking after a half dozen.

They didn't consider this a burden because DelFrances had become like family to them. She was not yet thirty, with only the Martoglios to lean on. She needed a social life, some degree of independence. She was trying hard to support her family, to better their lives. She got a job as a laboratory technician, and she took classes at Montclair State University. With Barbara's help she eventually sought legal aid to try to get child support from the two men who had fathered her girls, one of whom had spent time in jail.

There were times, though, when DelFrances had difficulties shouldering the burden. Once, succumbing to depression, she abandoned the children, who remained with the Martoglios for weeks. "When we sensed Del was stressed, we would help out more," Barbara said.

Things seemed to be stable in early 1997, though. The girls—nine, seven, and five—were all happily attending Northeast Elementary School in Montclair. DelFrances had earned a promotion at her job and was involved in a new relationship at work. And then came tragedy beyond belief.

Firemen responding to an early morning blaze at 127 North Fullerton on January 22, 1997, made a grisly discovery: three girls, dead from gunshot wounds, along with their mother, also killed by a gunshot wound to the head. The police immediately speculated (and months later confirmed) that DelFrances Bennett had taken the lives of her children with a .22 caliber pistol before turning it on herself. It was two days after her thirty-first birthday. The story rocked a community still recovering from a post office shooting that claimed four lives in March 1995. How could it happen? What on earth could have moved a mother to shoot her children?

In their inconsolable grief, this was a question Ed and Barbara tried to grapple with in a deeply personal way. The tragedy inevitably became another media event in the never-ending cycle of American gun violence. Reporters would descend on Montclair, and after some digging in the community would start phoning the Martoglio home. Ed and Barbara passed along to the weekly *Montclair Times* a heartbreaking photo of Barbara and DelFrances, on the porch of their home, with the six children (the Martoglios would soon after have a fourth).

No one would ever know what pushed DelFrances Bennett beyond the realm of reason. It was much too complicated, and too close to home, for the Martoglios to grope for answers. They knew DelFrances too well, had seen firsthand how hard she had struggled to rebuild her life. It was better not to dwell on the scattered pieces of this numbing puzzle.

For Barbara, the finality of four lives was perhaps comprehensible only in the context of women everywhere who found themselves in such predicaments, against overwhelming odds. She drew from it reinforcement for her belief that it was never too soon to begin developing a young girl's sense of entitlement and self-esteem. Years later she would wistfully recall how she occasionally tried to convince DelFrances to get the girls to play soccer, the athletic common denominator in town. Barbara was speaking from experience, appreciating the benefits she had derived from sports. As a social worker she felt it made perfect sociological sense that participation in sports for all girls could result in a healthier sense of self, and perhaps a greater degree of safety.

In 1997 the President's Council on Physical Fitness, under the direction of the Tucker Center for Research on Girls and Women in Sport at the University of Minnesota, had released an extensive study ("Physical Activity and Sport in the Lives of Girls") that supported this conviction. Girls involved in sports were more likely to have an enhanced sense of competence and control, and the report offered statistical evidence to support the widespread belief that athletics "can help many young girls avoid unwanted sexual activity and pregnancy." It also said that poverty "limits girls' access to physical activity and sport," especially for girls of color being raised by a single mother. While adding that extensive additional research was needed on the subject, the report posed a more complex question: "Does higher self-esteem fostered by sports help females to avoid inappropriately invasive males better than their nonathletic counterparts?"

To Barbara it seemed clear that, however the benefits of sport might express themselves under the clinical microscope, it couldn't hurt a girl to try. At the very least a sport like soccer offered beautiful mornings out in the park, away from the television and the computer, and served as a vaccine against the old-school view that, when it comes to the playing fields, girls should be ornamental objects who cheer on the boys.

Barbara didn't care if her young girls were all-stars, or any good at all; she just wanted them to try. She found it unsettling one day, driving back from the shore at the end of a long summer afternoon, when she asked her two daughters—eight-year-old Emily and seven-year-old Madeline—what sport they wished to try in the coming months. "I don't really want to join," Madeline said. "I just want to go shopping with you." Barbara thought, Oh, God, we're in trouble if that's what she thinks is an activity. She knew she needed a strategy, and soon.

"What if I were to coach: Would you do soccer?" she asked.

"Yes," Madeline said.

"I'd do it, too," said Emily.

Barbara, who knew nothing about soccer, soon found herself looking at a dozen seven- and eight-year-olds who were expecting pearls of wisdom from her.

Fortunately, her third-grade son, Richard, played soccer with John Ciardi. Thus the timing of Lisa's invitation could not have been more perfect. Barbara saw an opportunity to get some exercise outdoors, away from the Y, and to learn a few tricks she might teach the girls.

But soccer had also entered Barbara's life at a time when she had been longing for new social connections. "You know, you have your work relationships, and then you've got relationships that come from the children, the mothers you interact with because of play dates," she said. "But in my life, probably since college, there weren't a lot of friendships that evolved just because of someone I met on my own. You sort of don't want to work on it; you just want it to happen. So I got involved because I thought it would make me a better coach, but then it became something just for me."

Playing soccer did make her a better coach and a more involved mother—and it came at a time when she absolutely needed to be both. It was during the spring of Barbara's first league season that the Martoglios dealt with a new and very different kind of personal crisis. For some time Emily had been having painful headaches. After several rounds of examinations and tests, doctors broke the news that the Martoglios' daughter had been diagnosed with neurofibromatosis. The *Harvard Medical School Family Health Guide* describes the disease as "a group of rare genetic disorders that affect the skin and the nervous system and can cause mental retardation...[k] One form is characterized by benign (noncancerous) fibrous growths called neurofibromas that develop on the skin and the spinal cord. In other forms, the tumors occur in the eye and other organs and can sometimes be malignant."

There was a series of MRIs to determine the seriousness of Emily's case. The weeks of waiting for the various results dragged on like years. Barbara felt lucky to have soccer to share with her daughter. Fortunately, the tests revealed nothing malignant. "Through that whole period I'd come home and there would be three or four messages from different friends on the Belles," she said. "There was something great, something that made you feel secure, about having a whole group behind you."

Teamwork had taken on a whole new meaning for the Bluestone Belles. They were more than just friends for Barbara—as it had for Venera Gashi, the team became a second family. It was no wonder that the team photo meant so much to Barbara, more than a trophy ever could; the trophy represented the games, a compilation of plays, most of which would eventually blur together, while the photo was about the individuals who coalesced into a whole that was surely greater than the sum of its parts.

"We were the first soccer moms, and I don't care if we never win another game," Clare Moore said the night the Bluestone Belles won their championship, paraded into Tierney's, set their trophies on the bar, and ordered a celebratory round.

"I think we're going to grow old doing this," Venera told Lisa.

Three thousand miles away there were literally a couple of thousand women who would have raised their glasses to the very thought.

6

Role Models

JAN MCFADDEN was antsy, excited, clearly in a hurry to reach her destination. She groaned when her husband missed the exit off the highway. In the backseat she edged forward as if that might help navigate the car.

"You'll warm me up?" she asked.

Bill McFadden, more intent on finding the fastest route back toward the lights of the soccer pitch that were fading in the rearview mirror, only nodded.

"Course," he said.

Back in New Jersey the Montclair women would be indoors on this night, in the comforting warmth of the soccer dome. Here in downtown Seattle it was dark and dreary, early spring breaking out with its customary groan. No problem, as far as Jan was concerned. She had a game, and it would be played outdoors, and it didn't matter if the mist turned to rain and if the late-night chill became a teeth-chattering cold. In Seattle you played, rain or rare shine. You played even during the dead of winter, in what was affectionately known as the Frostbite League.

Jan McFadden had sat out the 1998–99 winter season, and now she was making a comeback after surgery to remove a bunion on her right toe and to implant several screws in her foot. She had played with pain for five years, until she could no longer scrape the front of her foot along the ground, a condition that made her pretty useless in goal—the position she most often had, and always with the same zealous pride.

She hated not playing soccer. It reminded her of the last time, back when she was working long hours for U.S. West and Bill suggested that she go cold turkey on the game, if only for a while, so they could spend more time together. He soon regretted that idea.

"I was so crabby that after a while he said, 'Jan, you've got to play soccer,'" she recalled.

So she returned to the playing fields, to her various teams in the open league and over-thirty and over-forty divisions, and wherever else she might find a game. Bill had long ago gotten with the program, doing a little coaching, befriending Jan's teammates, and accompanying her to many of the games in the area and the occasional tournament elsewhere in the state.

Bill, at sixty-six, was obviously at a different stage of life than Jan, who had just turned forty-eight. They did not have children (Bill's kids from a previous marriage were long grown and off in different parts of the country); he loved sports, but soccer was not his thing, never was, and never could be. When he was nineteen Bill had let a girlfriend drive his car, and they wound up slamming head-on into a truck. He suffered life-threatening internal injuries, and his right heel and big toe were destroyed. A tall man with a stiff walk, he was content to be on the sideline, puffing away on a cigarette, providing a running game commentary.

Occasionally Bill talked about moving south, to a more soothing climate, like San Diego's. But that would mean giving up the house with the lake view amid the pine splendor of the Seattle suburbs. More to the point, moving away would mean Jan giving up soccer— or at least soccer in Seattle, and the whole social scene that went along with it. Playfully, she would remind him of her favorite bumper sticker, a declaration of independence pasted on chrome that she had come across in her quarter century of playing the sport: MY HUSBAND SAYS HE'LL DIVORCE ME IF I PLAY ANOTHER SOCCER GAME. I'LL MISS HIM.

From the looks of things, Jan wouldn't have to carry her crusade that far. Bill knew what soccer meant to her; he understood her when she said, "I missed my childhood. I'm having it now."

She grew up near Portland, in Tigard, Oregon, athletic and bitter, always asking why there weren't teams for girls, prodding and push-ing for time in the gym. Through sheer will she and her friends managed a small measure of athletic activity, organizing informal volleyball and basketball games while school administrators more or less rolled their eyes.

In hindsight, she didn't blame them as much as she did the par-ents for not asking why fitness was not a priority for their daughters. The adults, especially those residing in her house, should have known better; her parents were both educators, and she could still recall debating the subject with her father when she was in junior high school. "Girls would lose interest," he'd say.

All these years later that argument made even less sense, Jan said, considering how her father had "worked so hard to get my older brother interested when he wasn't, and tried to force him into it. And here he had a bunch of girls who organized themselves, contacted other schools, had our mothers bring potluck dinners, wore our gym uniforms because there was no money, no fans, and no paid coaches. How could he say we weren't interested?"

Jan, who moved to Seattle in the mid-seventies, would not be stuck in the same sad cycle of athletic irrelevance for much longer. "When I first met her, she wasn't very friendly, and she went around with these dark circles under her eyes," Bill said. They met as co-workers at U.S. West. Jan was married to someone else, another Bill.

She had married Bill No. 1 and reluctantly left a gratifying job in Portland—in addition to her family and friends—because her husband wanted to pursue a doctorate at the University of Washington. They started house hunting, and Jan, a math major in college, found work in the engineering department at U.S. West (then Pacific Bell). She had to put in sixty hours a week, and that was a good week; she had little time for herself, no friends to fill it, no balance in her life—and after all that sacrifice, all that stress, Bill No. 1 quit school after a couple of months.

"Imagine how that played, after I'd left my family and friends so he could go to school," Jan said. "But he looked at his parents as role models, and once we got married, he thought he should have more money. I was used to living on a small budget, but he didn't like the idea that I was earning the money. He was always belittling my job."

Bill No. 1 got his own job and threw himself into it, which put them both on the corporate treadmill, trudging toward financial security and a nervous breakdown. And that was when Jan's headache started, except it was more than just the occasional ache; it was ongoing, practically a way of life. "I had it for six months," she said. "I was sick all the time—physically, emotionally. I couldn't sleep. I had nightmares. I was breaking out in cold sweats. I was fainting. I was at a low point in my life, very depressed, going downhill fast."

She tried swimming on a regular basis. She took a sewing class, a home decorating class, a skydiving course. Nothing made her feel better; nothing stimulated her interest or tapped into her passion, until someone mentioned a soccer league for women. She called the Parks Department and was given the number of the Washington State Women's Soccer Association.

One day, she recalls, she found herself on a makeshift field in a pair of cheap plastic cleats. "I got out there for the drills and I didn't know what I was doing and my feet hurt and I wasn't in shape and my lungs were burning," she said. And then, when the practice was over and she was dog tired, the realization set in, like a jolt of Starbucks caffeine, that her headache was gone. And every time she went back, it was as if she'd extracted the pain from her head and stored it in the glove compartment. For as long as she played, she was cured.

The coach, a Scottish immigrant named Alex Black, didn't treat her and the other beginners like a bunch of, well, girls: If they were going to play, then they were going to play the right way. Some of the women didn't appreciate the criticism, but Jan loved it, waiting to hear Alex call out her name, which meant she was doing something wrong, but, as she said, "Here was a man who didn't think, 'It's a bunch of girls and who cares if they do it right?'"

Encouraged by Jan to come share her new outlet, Bill No. 1 tried soccer, but not for long, eventually expressing annoyance at her growing involvement with her new team, which practiced as much as three times a week. Jan, playing center fullback, was still working long hours, but more and more she was beginning to cut corners, finding time to play. On game day, Saturday, she would often bolt from the field straight to the office. She was living for those surges of excitement, of freedom, that soccer was providing. She knew she was in a transitory stage of life in more ways than one.

Not surprisingly, her marriage to Bill No. 1 failed. And when Bill McFadden entered her life, and Jan began to develop an affinity for playing goal, he would spend hours with her on wet Seattle fields, because he remembered those dark circles under her eyes, and he had listened when she told him what had made them disappear.

Jan, at five-four, didn't have the classic goalie's body, and she wasn't the most natural and nimble athlete. But, like wisdom and self-esteem, some sports skills can be acquired. "I'd throw the ball in a puddle, and she'd dive," Bill said.

Wherever Jan would go, whatever team she would come across, it seemed someone always needed a goalie. People needed her, in the way she needed them, and it made her feel special, alive. She could walk onto a field, not know a soul, introduce herself to the fullbacks, the defenders, and make new friends.

Along the way Jan had been diagnosed with low blood sugar—which at least helped explain the fainting—and her doctors told her she needed to eat more. How many times when she was still working had she brought bananas and assorted snacks to the game, and set them behind her in the net, hoping her team would keep the ball down at the other end long enough for her to peel and munch?

She took to conducting goalie clinics for women—not for profit but to give back something for all the game had given her. She wrote a how-to pamphlet for women soccer beginners and printed copies out of pocket, giving them away. She played in the various age-groups at different skill levels, in pickup games and on elite tournament teams. She served on the board of the Washington State Women's Soccer Association and as manager for many of her teams, and she somehow found time to coach youth girls, too.

This life, the one she had begun to build since that first pain-relieving practice, had become so much easier the last couple of years, after she took Bill's advice and joined him among the professionally retired. Now, when Jan handed out her card, there was no trace of corporate America: just her name, address, and number, and a soccer ball in the top right corner. Now the evolution was complete: When she looked in the mirror every morning, she didn't see the old Jan, the one with the raccoon eyes; she saw the Jan who had jumped from that corporate treadmill to a life of moving forward, with the help of others.

That was the essence of the game, and her life. Soccer wasn't just part of it; it was "my entire social life," Jan said, to which Bill, sitting nearby, would snort, "Oh, thank you. Thank you very much."

He knew, though, that she was not exaggerating when she credited soccer with "resetting my priorities and restoring my health." And when Jan thought about it, she had no trouble at all admitting that soccer had virtually saved her life.

YOU HAVE NO IDEA how many women's lives soccer has changed," Bernadette Noonan said, armed not with statistics but with unwavering assurance. "Thousands, because all they did for so long was cook and take care of the kids." In her day the country was just going through the social and political convulsions that would accelerate the elevation of women in the workplace. Here, though, were Bernadette and her old friend, Janet Slauson, soccer soul mates who had taken their cause to the heart of the male sanctum. Before Title IX was much more than a piece of convoluted legislation, before there were celebrated role models and grassroots programs for girls, before the WNBA and the Women's World Cup, Bernadette and Janet stood up and said that they wanted to play. They wanted the field.

Their eyes twinkled as they shared a good laugh—the last laugh, you could say—when Bernadette recalled the male administrator who had told them, "Not in my lifetime." Oh, it was ages ago, and they were much younger (though they weren't volunteering specifics). They recounted the history sitting over fish and chips and ale in their favorite darkened pub, not far from Seattle's historic waterfront markets.

That they wouldn't give their ages didn't matter: They had raised their little ones back in the sixties and seventies, and it wasn't difficult to do the math. Like Jan McFadden, both had played through the decades, and it hadn't been easy to quit the game.

"My knees gave out," Bernadette said.

"My hip gave out," Janet said.

Their hearts still in, they weren't yet giving up the struggle, the cause, or control of the 140 teams in the far-flung Washington State Women's Soccer Association (WSWA). It wasn't the only well-developed soccer program for women (including older woman); there were serious leagues in Oregon and in Southern California, and they had a longtime rival in the Silicon Valley Soccer League from the San Francisco Bay Area. Teams of women over forty and over fifty from all around the country were meeting up for tournaments on a regular basis now—but their leagues, they believed, were the oldest, the largest, and the grandest. They were certain they had created the first league for women over thirty. The WSWSA now had several skill divisions for open play, over thirty, and over forty. They had eight over-fifty teams and were planning one for over sixty.

Upon hearing of the progress Lisa Ciardi and the Montclair women had made in a few short months, Bernadette teased her guest from New Jersey. "What took you so long on the East Coast?" she said. "You tell those women that they need to run their own league. Don't let a man do it. Men have their own way with sports, and we have ours."

This unyielding attitude had been solidified by years of struggle in a less accommodating era; an attitude born of being told, time and again, "You can't have the field because it's being used," when Bernadette knew for a fact that it was as open as a prairie. Of lugging portable goals to every game because her league had been relegated to a Little League baseball field. Of hiring male refs who thought it was beneath them and would stand in the middle of the field, guessing on calls at the far end in either direction.

But Bernadette and Janet—though still skirmishing—had won the war. The WSWSA had sixty-nine fields available to it across the Puget Sound area. Forty-two of the fields were equipped with lights. For seven dollars, a player could buy the WSWSA's "Which Pitch," a thick bound manual with directions and maps to every one of the fields.

Bernadette and Janet could operate with an open-door policy, a low-cost mandate, so no woman—executive or nanny—would be left out. Back in densely populated northern New Jersey, where good fields were sparse by comparison and the kids (and men) often came first, the Montclair moms had to take what they could get. They had to count on others to find a sympathetic figure. But while Ashley Hammond saw that encouraging the women was good business, he also strongly believed that they had as much right to play in the new dome as the men.

Every insurgency needs an ally, and, as a matter of fact, the first WSWSA president was also male. Mike Ryan went on to become the first U.S. Women's National Team coach after helping to make Seattle a hotbed for women's and girls' soccer activism.

It had all started so innocently, a bunch of mothers whose kids played, getting some exercise in the days before aerobics came into vogue, calling themselves the Hot Mamas and kicking the ball around every now and then. One of the women placed an advertisement in a shoppers' weekly, and a hundred women responded. Soon an official league was formed, with an unofficial credo that would have made Billie Jean King proud: "Ladies don't play soccer—women do."

At the time the Seattle Sounders were in the old North American Soccer League (NASL), which was embarking on a brief, popular run in several major U.S. markets. The Sounders ran a regular promotion offering half-price admission to kids in their soccer uniforms; the women showed up one day in uniform, demanding the bargain rate.

"We had a party after that first season," Bernadette said. "One of the husbands took home movies. We watched it and he said, 'You look like high school kids.' It was so much fun. I never had so much fun."

As a child, she never could have imagined soccer being a source of such pleasure. She grew up near Ireland's northern border, and in those politically charged towns soccer, considered an English game, was practically taboo. Standing on the sideline as a young mom, watching her children chase the ball, Bernadette was filled with guilt. It only got worse when she was the player. "I thought that if my mother knew what I was doing, oh, Jesus," she said. Too late, though; she was in America now, and she was hooked.

She had come to the States in the 1950s, visiting a cousin who taught school on the East Coast. They went west during the summer; the day she walked the streets of Seattle, she knew she was home. "It was like Ireland, rainy and green," she said. "On every hill, every street, I could see the water. I can feel it even now, the emotion I felt when I saw the water."

Janet was a Seattle girl who had grown with the city, from the Boeing bust to the Microsoft boom. She was a skier and field hockey player at the University of Washington who didn't get a varsity letter because, as she said, "they didn't give letters to girls."

When she started the WSWSA with Bernadette, they made up their own letters. They started with nine teams in 1974, expanded to thirty-six the next year and seventy-two the year after that. The association was very much on its way; with Mike Ryan at the helm, it produced national championship teams such as the Blue Angels, and the league set the early standards for women's excellence in soccer. They developed national team and world champion players: Amy

Allmann, goalie for the 1991 U.S. world champions, went on to coach at the University of Washington; Lori Henry and Shannon Higgins were also WSWSA players on that team. Michelle Akers, one of the 1999 World Cup cover girls, could trace her roots to women like Bernadette Noonan and Janet Slauson.

Though they relished working with players like Allmann and Akers, Bernadette and Janet found as much joy in the development of a Jan McFadden, of every apprehensive soul to whom they would patiently say, "Soccer is just passing the ball to someone on your team." They could go on forever, with stories about these women—their teammates and their peers. They could talk about women whose husbands had refused to give them money for soccer—"one husband told his wife, 'Take it out of the food money if it's so damn important,'" Bernadette said—so they said, The heck with that, and got their own jobs to pay their way. They could tell you about Lynn Nutt, who fell in love with and married a ref. And then there was Jean Wilcoxen, whose family story was as sweet a tale as any mother could tell.

Jean was a throwback, one of the originals, who began playing in the early seventies, before the births of her daughters, Tracy and Farah. The girls were practically raised on a soccer pitch, introduced to the sport by watching Mom tear up the field. Jean coached them when they were young, and they became good enough to play in high school and college.

At Highline Community College, Farah was a sophomore and Tracy a freshman when fall soccer practice began in 1997. The team, because of injuries and transfers, was a couple of players short. The Wilcoxen sisters put their heads together and came to the conclusion that three were better than two. They volunteered their mother, and while Jean would agree only to give it some thought, her daughters "borrowed" her credit card and enrolled her for twelve credits at night.

Jean, a 1967 high school graduate, already working half days as a staff supervisor at an elementary school, had years ago played with her two sisters and had the time of her life. She realized that playing on a team with her daughters was a mother's sports fantasy. Someday when she was old and sedentary and smiling at the mere thought of soccer, these would be the best memories of all.

Her husband, Stan, agreed to her final conditions: He promised to do the vacuuming, the laundry, the dishes, and dinner while Jean enrolled in computer and psychology courses. She went to her first practice and was introduced to the team as its newest player, the forty-eight-year-old freshman sweeper. Even the players on the team she hadn't diapered soon took to calling her Mom.

Farah, the captain, relished keeping Jean in position—and in line. "Sort of a role reversal," she said, while admitting that her mother seldom needed instructional discipline or even much help keeping up with players who were more than a quarter century younger. Jean more than held her own; she was selected for the conference all-star game.

"She rocks," Farah told an interviewer at the time, though Jean said she drew the line when they asked her to roll.

"They'd go out dancing," she said, two years later. "I'd go home to my husband."

Through the years Bernadette and Janet had heard and shared so many inspirational stories. Not to be discounted, they insisted, were the true triumphs of everyday family life. Ann Rackers, one of the over-fifties players, and her husband had years ago joined a coed recreation team and made soccer their regular Friday night date. Sue Boettcher took up soccer as an adult and wound up making a career out of it, as a high school coach. Pat Tuton, who had plenty of opportunities to play growing up in the affluent New York City suburb of Bronxville, had been coaching women's soccer teams for years and said, "I've never had a player say, 'I've got menstrual cramps, I can't run.'"

As a counselor of women who abused themselves and often could not find the strength to get out of bed, Pat often preached the benefits of being connected to a support group via sports. You learned toughness and discipline and commitment—though Bernadette and Janet agreed that the older women tended to celebrate these benefits to a greater extent than did the younger ones, who more and more took team life for granted, just like the boys. They were less likely to take on the job of team manager, to organize the roster and line the field. But Bernadette and Janet believed that should be part of the process, too. Sports should not be taught the way today's indulged young athletes often learn it; it is not just an entitlement but an experience, and to get the most out of it you have to share it, be involved in it.

This was their sports model, anyway—"our way," as Bernadette had put it—and was the legacy she and Janet and now Jan, one of their star protégées, wished to pass on. So they prodded and pushed and gave out awards—the Bernadette Noonan Award, for example—for volunteer service. They held fund-raisers and undertook time-consuming endeavors like the annual Linda Adams Memorial Tournament, named for one of the players they had lost to cancer.

They had come such a long way, but they never wanted to forget how they started, taking apprehensive first steps, and receiving gentle shoves. "I've literally helped thousands of women find a team, a new family," Bernadette said.

"I always wanted to write on a bathroom wall, 'For a good time, call Bernadette,'" Janet cut in, the two old friends cracking up again.

For the twenty-fifth anniversary season, kicking off in spring 1999, more than 2,500 women had dialed their number—which only proved, after all these years, that Bernadette and Janet were still Hot Mamas. "We gave birth," Bernadette said, Janet nodding in agreement, and Jan smiling like their proud daughter. "And boy, are we proud."

• • •

STILL AN HOUR AWAY from her 8:30 game time, Jan began her stretching along the sideline. The field, empty except for a father kicking a ball with his young son near the far goal, was mostly sand, a surface more accommodating for Seattle's wet climate, and also more forgiving to a goalie hurling herself to the ground. The game was in the Georgetown section of Seattle, an old neighborhood with a fraying, industrial feel. Off in the distance, beyond the field, a cargo train lumbered through, its rumble mingling with the steady rush of freeway traffic.

"Who's playing tonight?" Bill asked, as Jan strapped on her shin guards and slipped a wool band over her short brown hair and down over her ears. This was an independent open league, not affiliated with the WSWSA, and thus, Jan explained, it tended to be less organized, more of a pickup experience. Jan was playing only because she needed the activity to work off the rust from her injury and inactivity.

"I'm not even sure—I don't really know all the players on this team," she said. "I know Patty's coming late because it's her son's birthday and she won't leave until he's asleep."

"Oh, wait until you see Patty," Bill told a guest. "She's really something."

While Jan was stretching, the temperature kept dropping, probably down to around forty degrees. The wind, whipping through the open acreage, made the night feel at least ten degrees colder.

A couple of other players, women at least twenty years younger than Jan, arrived and began stretching about fifty yards away. Now Jan picked up a ball and tossed it to Bill. He let it settle onto his left arm and cradled it against his chest. He dropped the cigarette he was holding between his right middle and index fingers and stamped out the butt. Together, they walked out to the nearest goal.

Jan assumed her stance. Bill, in front, began tossing the ball to the ground. Jan dove: first left, then right. Left. Right.

Another train rumbled past. Behind the fence a couple more cars pulled up. The father and son were still kicking down at the far end. Now Bill, hands in the pockets of his jacket, took a slow walk to the center of the field and turned around to face Jan back near the goal. He raised his right hand.

Jan strode into the ball and punted it high into the air. It bounced, a few feet in front of Bill, off to his right. In a stiff-legged trot he gave chase and bent to scoop it up. Now he set the ball in front of him, as if holding it up on a tray. And then, leveraging off the heel that was irreparably damaged so many years before, Bill powered into the ball with his big, toeless right foot.

It sputtered like a wounded quail and bounced unthreateningly back toward Jan before rolling to a stop. She picked up the ball and waited. Bill returned to the middle and signaled for his wife to punt it again.

7

Hitting Home

T HE CALL CAME IN to Beth Fuqua one spring day from the friend of an old college pal. Did she by some chance happen to remember Linda Zalkauskus? Now Linda Hahn, she had read a newspaper story about these soccer-playing mothers in Montclair. She recognized one of the names and called her friend. "I think I went to college with her," she said. "You ought to give her a call."

Regina Nejman, who had fished Beth's number out of the telephone directory, was a soccer player, too. She was not yet a mother, but she had been walking in Riverside Park on Manhattan's Upper West Side one evening when she came upon a bunch of women chasing a ball. Regina stopped to watch, casually mentioning how she, young enough at thirty to have reaped the benefits of Title IX, had played the game from the time she was a kid. These women were older, several of them well into their forties, and a couple past fifty. But they were so friendly, and so determined—and they were so, um, in need of a good soccer trainer.

Though the competition was unexceptional, Regina figured that if this was where the action was, she might as well get on out there and play. But that was almost four years ago, much had occurred since then, and, well, she and her friends were wondering if the Montclair mothers would be interested in playing a game—a "friendly," in the parlance of the sport. "We didn't know there were any other women in the area like us," Regina said.

By this point the women from the big city were calling themselves the Parlour Moms, for their sponsor, the Parlour, an Irish pub and restaurant on the Upper West Side. This was where they often retreated after their first evening practices; John Kelly, the Parlour's co-owner, could recall them stumbling into the bar, tired, dirty, and frustrated. A year later they had hand-me-down uniforms from their children, and the Parlour Moms were so much improved that they won a championship in the Bronx Irish League—a decade-old association founded by newly arrived immigrants and now composed mainly of teams from the Bronx and Queens.

The Parlour Moms' first game was a 9–0 rout in the driving rain, but four years can make for an enormous amount of progress; now they were good enough and confident enough and adventurous enough to be planning another Irish invasion, a summertime trip to Ireland for a series of games against other amateur teams.

While a "friendly" sounded exhilarating, Beth Fuqua wanted Regina to understand that the Montclair women were not quite ready for the international circuit. The mere thought of playing an experienced team, with a full complement of eleven players who actually adhered to the offside rule, was likely to cause some pre-match indigestion for several of the New Jersey women.

Not to worry, Regina said; the Parlour Moms' average age was forty-five, and from what Linda Hahn had told her about the Montclair women, their experience sounded like her team's Riverside Park days all over again. In other words, the Parlour Moms could relate.

Their founder was Joan Madden-Peister, a State Supreme Court judge who was past her fiftieth birthday when she set up a mothers' sign-up table in the corridor outside her sons' soccer awards ceremony. Joan had never played on a soccer team, or any kind of team, and had been moved to organize one only after years of presiding over the athletic lives of her sons, who were then fifteen and eleven. "I can't tell you how many hundreds of games I had gone to," she said. "And I always wanted to go out and kick a ball."

She agreed it was more whim than vision; after more than one hundred women signed the sheet, Joan took it home and deposited it in the folder marked "Wishful Thinking." One of her sons' coaches had warned her that it wouldn't be easy to start a team. How many women your age could find the time? he had asked. Where would you play? Who would organize and train you? There was a difference between kicking a ball around the park and playing soccer, and the coach had raised questions that were far more difficult to answer than to pose—at least until Wendy Hollender, one of the women who had signed the sheet, called one day and wanted to know whatever had happened to that soccer team idea?

Joan did not know Wendy, who was forty at the time, a partner in her own home-furnishing and design business, and the mother of soccer-playing children. Wendy had always been athletic, but more in individual sports; she jogged, skated, and played her share of tennis. She had taken an all-day soccer-coaching clinic and considered it one of the greatest days she'd had in years. She could still recall the rush of adrenaline she'd felt the moment the ball touched her foot. "I could do this," she said, though she realized that there was no one (at least no one she could think of) to do it with.

Joan quickly learned a few things about Wendy. First of all, she was a supreme and determined organizer, which was crucial to their hope of going forward. When she set her mind to something, the chances were it was going to get done. "Wendy became the motivating force," Joan said.

Wendy called a meeting for those who had signed Joan's sheet. About fifty women gathered in the north meadow of Central Park. Within a couple of months there were four teams conducting drills and playing informal games in Riverside Park.

When their ranks were depleted by the inevitable start-up injuries and because the commitment required time and energy that some simply did not have, the core women refused to give up the chase. They decided to abandon the struggle for a league of their own and to join one that was already established. They began playing downtown at Chelsea Piers, against much younger women, who looked at them as if they had all gotten lost on the way to the Volvo dealer.

They lost their first game, Wendy recalled, "by something like 20–3." Soon after they discovered the more welcoming Bronx Irish League, which conducted games in Van Cortlandt Park in the Bronx or on Randalls Island on Saturdays. That had been, for most of these women, a day more typically spent on the sideline watching their kids, but conflicting schedules be damned, they decided: They were determined to stop competing vicariously, and to start winning for themselves.

Wendy found them a trainer, and not just any trainer: Kevin McCarthy, who coached the Columbia University women's team. He had handled some of the kids' elite travel teams; "What about us?" Wendy asked him. McCarthy agreed to run weekly sessions for the Parlour Moms. They went out to the Hamptons to soccer camp, where Kevin trained them every day, except the morning after he took them on a pub crawl in Sag Harbor near his summer home.

The Parlour Moms kept getting better. They took on a few younger women. They integrated a goalie who had played in college, and when they won the Bronx Irish League championship in only their second season, they did it the way Brandi and Briana would eventually win the World Cup in the summer of 1999—on penalty kicks.

For Wendy, swift as she was small (she was barely five feet) and blessed with a strong left-footed kick, this had felt like the natural way to proceed. Others would have preferred to remain on more secure footing, playing only with one another. Joan, for instance, was a decade older, and was picking up the skills at a much slower rate. She became less certain of herself at her midfield position, trying to keep up with the younger, more aggressive and demanding women; she worried that she was holding the team back. Her husband kidded her that she "could be their mother." Some of her longtime friends wondered if she'd lost her mind.

"I loved playing, though, right from the start," Joan said. "There was a joyfulness about it that made me feel like a kid again. Kick a ball—isn't that what five-year-olds do?

"But on any team, tensions develop. Over the years our team has had excellent relationships, but there have been issues, particularly surrounding the skill levels—playing time and touches on the ball. I would have thought that, being in law, I would have been able to not allow my emotions to come into it. But out on the field, it was not easy at my age to develop the ball skills with my feet. You want to be part of it. You want to keep going. But there were times I would feel frustrated and discouraged. So many times, but then, especially over the last year or so, I would just look up the field and see Wendy.

"I'd look at her and think about what she was going through and how she was persevering. More than anything or anyone, Wendy became my inspiration, my source of strength."

"It's not an easy game to play, but you can improve," Wendy said. "We were never taught strategy in sports, but we began to learn things intellectually, to understand that there's a plan. It's a true challenge, but when it comes together, it's amazing."

Her husband, Jim Goldfarb, was often left behind as the lone parent on duty for the kids' Saturday games. Wendy still made it her business to get to as many of Abby's and Jesse's games as she could, just not when she had her own. Those games were her priority because this was her time, her last chance before middle age carried her to a place where she had no intention of going quietly. "You pour so many years into raising your kids and rushing around to work, and then one day you wake up and you feel so tired," she said. "In our generation we all watched our parents reach middle age and grow old, and what kind of message are you giving to your child? Middle age is not old age. Something happened when I was turning forty, the need to take care of not only the psychological but the physical."

She had never enjoyed working out in a gym, but she began lifting weights because she didn't want to get pushed around by younger women who were bigger, stronger, and just waiting for her to dribble their way. Wendy could always run, but now she could keep running until even the younger women would give up the chase. And when they did, when she beat them to the ball and slipped one past the goalie into the net, she felt younger, faster, fitter, and more alive than ever.

And then, suddenly, there came an opponent she could not dribble around or run away from. The doctors found a lump in her breast, and her world was radically changed, leaving her no choice but to promise herself she would not let it be destroyed.

•   •   •

WHEN SHE WAS diagnosed with cancer, Wendy naturally thought first about the children. "I did not want my kids' lives to change," she said. She had seen this insidious by-product of a parental illness firsthand, how a family's infrastructure could be devastated by the belief that a parent was no longer whole; Wendy was determined not to let that happen. In September 1998, while Lisa Ciardi was collecting signatures in Montclair, the women in the Bronx Irish League were taking up a collection for Wendy, stuffing crumpled and dusty bills into a white envelope. This was an old custom from the Potato Famine days, the community caring for one of its own.

Though never in denial, Wendy was determined to get on with her life, and that life included soccer. She didn't want to be taken care of by her teammates, she wanted to play ball with them. "Somehow, the thought of not being able to play was almost as devastating to me as getting cancer," she said. So the scars from her first surgery had barely begun to heal when Wendy asked her doctor, "When can I play?"

He thought she was joking, but she wasn't. Her husband got nervous, but she promised to be careful. Some of her teammates thought she wasn't thinking clearly, but she assured them she was. When one doctor, an older man, strongly advised against it, Wendy kept asking others until she finally got the answer she wanted.

Her teammates worried, with good reason, that she would be slide-tackled at the wrong time, even in practice. And what, exactly, were they supposed to do about the games? Make an announcement to the opponents, reminding them that their left-footed striker had recently had a mastectomy and to please, please take it easy on her? Wendy would kill them. The whole point of being there was that she wanted normalcy. She just wanted to play.

"After the biopsy and mastectomy, at practice, she owned the ball," Regina Nejman said. "We weren't going to challenge her. We'd say, 'Are you sure you should be playing?'"

"I'm playing," Wendy would say.

She played on, whenever she could, but her ordeal was just beginning. Six months of chemotherapy awaited her. Six weeks of radiation. More surgeries, including the removal of her ovaries, after which she sat up in her hospital bed and announced, "I've got a game in five days."

While the doctors marveled at the shape she was in, at her low body fat, the chemotherapy created a new set of issues. It could cause her blood counts, including her platelets, which promote clotting, to fall, they said. If she continued to play, there was always the possibility that she could get bruised, start bleeding, and not stop. Wendy knew the risk and didn't mean to be reckless; she suggested having her platelets checked every week, the day before her game. The doctors looked at each other and shrugged. What were they going to do with this woman, who was creating her own program for maintaining a positive attitude in the face of life-threatening crisis? "It just got to the point where they said, 'You know your own body,'" she said.

She thought she did, anyway. She took a knee to the midsection in one game and felt a sharp pain. She shrugged it off and kept on going, and a couple of weeks later she was undergoing a bone scan when the doctor said, "Do you realize that you have two broken ribs?"

"I do?" she said.

"Maybe," the doctor said, "you should take a couple of weeks off."

"It's too late now," Wendy said, laughing, and her point was that playing soccer, letting loose, had allowed her to develop a much higher threshold for pain, and for all the medical trauma she would have to withstand.

There were days, of course, when reality intruded. She would show up to practice and try to run but not be able to for more than a few minutes. Sometimes her teammates would substitute her in just for a corner kick; other times she would remain on the sideline, cheering and coaching, never complaining.

When her hair fell out as a result of the treatments, she sensed that her son was taking it especially hard. She decided that she had to be up front about this, to convince him and the others that she may look different but she was still Mom, still running. Right through Central Park she would jog, once or twice with a soccer ball at her feet, on her way across town to Mount Sinai Hospital for another round of chemo. Her attitude was and had to be that it was just another appointment, not her day's focal point; her life was going on, as planned.

"You could see at times that she was tired, feeling the effects of the radiation and medication," said Joan Madden-Peister. "But remaining with the team was more than just soccer; it was a different kind of bond that develops. We all wanted to be there for her. She was strong, so strong, but everyone needs support in a situation like that."

Wendy needed more than support; she needed outlets, because she was not willing to concede that life as she had known it was over, even with the surgeries and the early onset of menopause caused by the treatments. As much as Wendy needed love, she also needed life's little news briefs, a pick-me-up as simple as the score of the most recent game.

How could she ever forget that Saturday, back in the hospital for another surgery, when the Parlour Moms, in their latest green and white unis, came down the hallway, tracking mud and a phalanx of alarmed hospital personnel, with the report of that day's game?

How could she ever thank Karen Lindsey and the others who rolled up their sleeves and donated blood? Or Jane Kenney, who baked bread for her every week and promised to do so for as long as

Wendy was undergoing treatment. Whenever she concluded another round of chemo, her teammates were there with a cake, a pair of earrings, chicken soup and books. They sat with her on the sideline when she tired at practice, and dragged her out dancing when her strength returned. "They didn't treat me like an invalid," Wendy said. "When I played, they expected me to perform."

This was teamwork at its ultimate level, the fundamental and most high-minded lessons of the playing field applied passionately and generously to real life.

Wendy was without question the Parlour Moms' leader and guiding spirit. She had pretty much talked her friend and business partner Celia Reiss into joining and staying on the team, despite Celia's belief that she was and is the weakest player. "Wendy just has that drive," Celia said, "and I would look at her and think, Is that what makes the real athlete? Is it just because she wants it more?"

It sounds like every cliché mouthed by a millionaire athlete or coach, but in Wendy's case the results spoke for themselves.

"I've always felt that women who have families and careers really have two jobs," Celia said. "And that's what has made this team so special, having women support each other, being strong, in control. It's why I haven't given up the darn thing, even though I'm so pathetic."

She did wonder if the team's response would have been as poignant and profound if the stricken member had been anyone other than Wendy. Wendy believed most assuredly it would have been—and if not, then the Parlour Moms weren't what she fancied them to be.

It was a group that believed in whatever it was doing, wherever it was going, be it Shelter Island for a team getaway during the summer of '98 or the coming extravaganza in Ireland in midsummer 1999. "I'm fifty years old, and it doesn't seem like a valid thing because it seems very selfish and separate from my family and work, but it's mine," said Maggie Bradley-Cook, a physical therapist who had played basketball in high school and run a 4:04 New York City Marathon in 1979. Her teenage daughter had played soccer in Denmark and Sweden the previous summer, and Maggie was intrigued. She arranged the Ireland trip through contacts in the Bronx Irish League. Not all the Parlour Moms could commit the time, so they recruited a few single women from a competing team, the Harps. But Joan and Celia and Jane Kenney were all in. So, of course, was Wendy, and none of them flinched upon learning they would be facing teams of much younger women in Dublin and Galway, and on larger fields than they were accustomed to.

Who could have imagined Joan's sign-up table would lead to this? How often, Celia asked herself as she considered leaving her young children behind with her husband, would women like her get the chance to jet off on a trip like this? For Wendy there was never a question about going, no doubt that her participation was meant to be. And when the Parlour Moms decided to discard their green-and-white uniforms for a set of jazzier hand-me-downs from the kids, the sponsor's name stitched on the shirts only reinforced that belief. MIRACLE HOUSE, they said.

Miracles were, understandably, on Wendy's mind. A few days before the Parlour Moms would leave for Ireland, Lena Williams of *The New York Times* wrote a feature story about their trip. It ran on the paper's front sports page, alongside the inspirational saga of Lance Armstrong, the American cyclist who had just finished a rousing victory in the Tour de France after a bout with testicular cancer not long before. "If I had read about him three years ago, I would have said, 'That's impossible,'" Wendy said.

But now the possibilities seemed limitless. The world was opening up to her in an entirely new way. Wendy's chemotherapy treatments had ended; her dark, curly hair was beginning to grow back. She had been running through a long, dark tunnel and was now emerging into a dazzling light, onto a succession of lush, green fields, the most perfect soccer pitches she had ever walked on. "Like putting greens," she said, pointing them out while turning the pages of her photo album from the trip.

How amazing it had felt to play there, she said, for the Parlour Moms to be like their World Cup idols, ambassadors of sport and international goodwill. How joyous it was for Wendy to be with her teammates, her friends, out to dinner and at the theater, around the countryside or in the pubs. They toasted their hosts, and each other; the older, authentic Parlour Moms raised their glasses of Guinness to the young women who had come with them; and they all toasted their success after winning two of the four games.

Most of all, they drank to Wendy, their inspiration, who in the last game put on a dazzling offensive show, scoring all three of the Parlour Moms' goals in a 3–2 send-off victory. And when she really thought about it, when she let herself swell with satisfaction and pride, Wendy knew there was nothing miraculous about the goals, the trip, or her. The entire experience could only be explained and understood as a victory of the spirit, an affirmation of life.

THE MONTCLAIR MOTHERS formed their team for the scrimmage against the Parlour Moms—the travel team, they joked—with players mostly from the Bluestone Belles and Poké-moms. They didn't want to make a big deal out of it. It wasn't as if they even intended that Sunday morning at Brookdale Park to keep score.

Except someone always does, and though no one would later remember the exact count, the unanimous recollection was that the Parlour Moms won by two or three goals. The Montclair moms held their own—not surprising, given the natural athleticism and rapid skill development of Lisa, Venera, and Jeanne Jeffrey, among others. Joan Madden-Peister could instantly tell which of the Montclair women were naturals, like Wendy, and which ones would likely struggle with this game, just as she had. She almost wanted to pat the backs of the ones she could better relate to, tell them not to get discouraged, to hang in there. "I felt a camaraderie there, something we don't usually feel playing in the Irish League," Joan said. "It's always collegial with the young ones, but there was something different, encouraging, about playing other mothers."

The Montclair women were more impressed that the Parlour Moms had full uniforms, played their eleven positions smartly, and understood how one wound up offside. This was all still very new to them, and sometimes the ball and the game went by in a blur.

"All I remember is that the coach kept yelling at someone named Celia," Dana DiMuro said. "It was, 'Come on, Celia,' and 'Celia, what the hell are you doing out there?'" The coach was Scott Greenberg, the boyfriend of one of the Parlour Moms. He had played soccer, but, according to Wendy, he tended to have more of the American football-marine mentality—yell enough and the player will eventually do as she's told out of pure fear. Scott volunteered his time, though, and the more sensitive Parlour Moms—even Celia, his favorite target—had learned to tune him out when they absolutely had to.

Dana, overcome by empathy, didn't know this and finally yelled out, "Would you just leave poor Celia alone already?" Everyone had a good laugh, and they later lined up, just like their kids, to shake hands.

"They had a nice level of fitness and skill," Wendy said. "What they lacked more than anything was how to play outdoors, positioning, formations. But they certainly were further along than we were our first year. It would be very interesting to play them again in another year."

On the morning Wendy played in Montclair, she was still undergoing chemotherapy, and because she didn't have hair, she wore a kerchief on her head. As always she hadn't wanted to be conspicuous for anything other than her play. She didn't know these women, and they, in turn, had no reason to suspect that the head covering was anything more than a fashion statement.

They would eventually know Wendy Hollender's story. They would all meet again under very different terms, with a far more elevated and enlightened definition of *team*. But first the Montclair moms had some catching up to do, some growing pains to suffer, and many more kinks to work out.

8

Generations

CHARLIE MCEWAN'S phone rang one day, his daughter Jen calling with some news from up around the Montclair area, where she worked as a hospice nurse. "Dad, they got something going on here," she said. "It's older women, lawyers' wives. They're so bad. They put me on a team that's awful, absolutely awful."

Jen playing soccer with lawyers' wives? That, Charlie thought, was a good one. She was the baby in the McEwan family, after his two boys, whom he'd trained to be soccer players almost from the time they could walk. Of course, whatever Scott and Stewart did, Jen had to do, too—including soccer, which Charlie had been raised in Scotland years ago to believe was a male sanctum, end of story.

"Oh boy," he'd said when his feisty little girl—who eventually grew up to be not so little—decided she was going to play, just like the guys. And play she did, because times were changing, and so Charlie had one very good reason to change along with them. Not only did Jen make the Kearny High School team but she became a mainstay of the new girls teams growing out of Charlie's fairly famous Thistle Football Club, named for a sponsoring fish 'n' chips joint in Kearny, New Jersey, an old mill town ten miles west of New York.

She played with the trademark McEwan intensity, and she wore Number 2 in the tradition of her brothers, though Charlie had to admit that Jen's soccer exploits had never seemed to matter quite as much to him. That was the old die-hard Scotsman in him, and maybe the new chauvinist Yank. Anyway, how could he possibly equate the two levels, the disparate worlds, when he and his sons had been part of something wonderful in his adopted country, a grass-roots American awakening to the Beautiful Game?

It was twenty years ago now, though it seemed like yesterday. Kearny's reputation as a soccer hotbed—traceable to an invasion of Scottish immigrants dating as far back as the mid-1870s—had been elevated by the Thistle club, because Charlie had literally pulled ethnic kids, immigrant kids, off the playgrounds of blue-collar Kearny and other hardscrabble places like Harrison and Newark. He gave these boys a place to narrow their athletic focus, harness their aggression, hone their skills. "Some of them were dirtbags, dirty players," Jen had to admit, but Charlie always contended the soccer pitch was no country club. If he was going to make players out of raw kids, push them out into the big, bad, developed soccer world, then better to begin with kids whose inferior skills would not be further limited by timid souls.

"My preference was always the European game, a different type of game from what our kids had been exposed to," he said. In the late 1970s and early 1980s, Charlie would import stalwart youth teams like the Glasgow Celtic Boys Club and jam two or three kids into each of his players' homes. Fifteen hundred spectators would ring the fields to watch the Scottish kids run the American teenagers ragged.

The Scottish players "were actually high-school-age signed professionals," he said. "They'd get what they called S forms, school forms, from the pro teams. They were so far ahead of our kids. They'd beat us 8–0, 9–1." But Charlie's Thistle teams—always scheduled last on the Glasgow boys' tour—began to inch closer, skill by skill, goal by goal, until finally they sent the Scottish lads home one year trophy-less and in shock. Charlie could still hear himself consoling the Glasgow coach, "Frank, our kids are getting better. It's got to happen."

More than a decade later, millions of Americans would come to know Charlie's best players, pulling for Tab Ramos and John Harkes and Tony Meola in the greatest sporting event on earth, the World Cup, on American soil. Ramos was "barely off the boat" from Uruguay in nearby Harrison when Charlie found him. Meola, the self-described "fat kid they stuck in goal," was the son of Vincent, who came to the States from Avellino when he was eighteen.

As far as Charlie was concerned, all his kids had done him proud—him and Kearny and every Scotsman who ever toiled in the mills operated by Clark Thread and Nairn Linoleum and played recreationally along the banks of the Passaic River. His club had done much to make Kearny "Soccer Town, U.S.A.," as the sign on Kearny Avenue read.

The Thistle club carried on, without Charlie these days. He'd had enough, done his share. He was content now to help out with his grandkids' teams, though he could tell that the fathers of the next generation—with dreams of college scholarships—would occasionally look at him and think, "Does this old man even know what he's doing?"

Jen, more than most, knew that Charlie McEwan did. Charlie—and her brothers—represented a legacy that was not always easy to live up to, though not for lack of effort. Even at twenty-nine, having played no organized soccer for almost a decade, Jen was trying, whenever possible, to pull herself up to the boys' level in the eyes of her dad. She still wanted to get his attention with what the McEwans were known for, the clean, perfectly timed slide tackle.

Why, just recently Charlie and his wife, Joyce, had driven from Kearny to Nutley to watch Jen play in a game composed of coaches from the youth league she volunteered in. Jen, the only female on the field, went after a guy dribbling down the sideline near where Charlie was standing. For what could have been only a millisecond, she made eye contact with her father, who glanced at Joyce as if to say, "Uh oh, she's at it again."

Jen, tall and strong, took the guy down, then awaited the judicial verdict that could not be appealed. "Good job," Charlie said afterward. "Very clean."

Poor Jen, he thought after getting off the phone the night she'd called. Lawyers' wives? She won't last two games.

But she did. "She called back a couple of weeks later," he said. "She says, 'I love it. I absolutely love it. These women—they're so bad, so bad, but you know something? They're getting better. And they're having fun. You've got to come up.' I said, 'Ahh, come on . . .'"

As fate would have it, Charlie had only recently been hit with bad news, some cancer cells that had to be addressed. The treatment was upcoming, and Joyce said, "Go on, it'll be good for you." They decided to see for themselves what Jen was talking about. Her new team, the Pride, was playing one Wednesday night at the Soccer Domain in a part of upscale Montclair that had more of an industrial edge, a Kearny feel. It was exactly what she had described—a few young soccer players in a fragile coexistence with the "lawyers' wives."

Jen introduced her parents to everyone, including the team's captain, Lori McNamara, a small, athletic blonde with a ponytail and a second-grader, Casey, in tow. Lori, not shy, invited Charlie to come teach the Pride a few pointers on a Saturday morning in Brookdale Park. Before he knew it this man who had developed World Cup players was calling the shots for the Pride against that international powerhouse the Pokémoms.

"The first couple of games, they'd stand on the sidelines, afraid to say a word," Charlie said. "I'd say, 'I need you to play here, do this,' and they'd look at me and say, 'Oh, I can't do that.' Then I went into the hospital for treatment and had to miss a couple of weeks, and here comes a bouquet of flowers from the team. I'm thinking, These are such nice women, but how are they ever going to become soccer players? Then I go back a few weeks later and they're yelling and screaming, and the one girl we put in goal is diving on everything and they're actually fighting over playing time."

Charlie couldn't get over it: a soccer league with a provision for the referee to yellow-card a player whose child was misbehaving on the sideline. "Oh, it's been years since I completely changed my thinking about girls playing the game," he said. Girls, mothers—what difference did it make? Their enthusiasm was energizing. Those mornings with them in the park, every word he said had the impact of gospel, and all over the surrounding fields were dozens of kids playing his game.

He coached a few more games for the Pride, then gave in to the demands of keeping up his strength while remaining on the job at the Pfister Chemical plant. Charlie had set the Pride on their way, and he felt good about it, except for one nagging thought. "These women have children to send to school in the morning—take it easy," he told Jen. Charlie didn't remember his daughter's answer, though a lifetime of experience made him reasonably certain it was unlikely she would do as he said.

· · ·

YOUR INSTINCTS take over in the heat of a game, in the urgency of the moment. So Wendy Cogdell's natural reaction when Beth Fuqua broke out of the pack in her defensive end with daylight ahead was to make sure the ball didn't get past midfield.

Wendy's team, the Pride, was already losing to the Pokémoms, 2–1, and was pressing for a tie. There could not have been more than five minutes left. Wendy, having moved up from her defensive position as the Pride controlled the play, trying to rifle the tieing goal past Nina Sloan, now made a beeline across the field, straight for Beth.

It was all Beth could do to keep control of the ball while moving forward as quickly as she could. Peripheral vision does not come easily to any new player. She never saw Wendy coming.

Wendy slid, targeting the ball. Down went Beth, rolling over, crying out in pain. She grabbed her right ankle, but from the way she screamed, her teammates were certain it was broken.

"It was the one I'd sprained badly years ago in college," Beth said. "It was worse then, but this time half of it was pain and half of it was just furious anger that somebody had done this to me." Somebody from another generation whom she didn't know and whose tactics she couldn't relate to.

The perpetrator had been a wisp of a woman, with long, wavy brown hair and a lilting Texas accent that made any serious act of aggression seem incongruous, if not downright impossible. Yet Wendy, twenty-five, had played the game as a kid and on through high school. She had been taught from the start to play hard.

Wendy had heard about the new league in the most unlikely way, standing at the train station heading to work in New York. The nice woman who owned the pasta restaurant alongside the tracks was sipping coffee and complaining about soreness from soccer the previous night. "Soccer?" Wendy had asked Sue O'Donnell, and that was all it took, because a woman who had grown up with the game did

Lisa Ciardi stretched her imagination and set her sights on creating a sports vehicle for soccer moms who no longer wanted to be confined to the sidelines.

Early days in the park: The group was small, but everyone had a ball. That's Beth Panucci dribbling in the foreground.

Knocked to the ground, Clare Moore reaches for a helping hand. Cathy Wright (*nearest to ball*) and Dana DiMuro, with their eyes trained on the ball, get on with the game.

Ellen Paretti smiles for the camera as Ginger Steuart, left, and Cathy Wright carry her off, but a severely sprained ankle would sideline her for weeks and create child care problems at home.

Television commercial producer Nina Sloan had never played team sports, but had natural talent as a goalie.

Venera Gashi, center, learned the game by playing with her brothers as a young Albanian immigrant in Brooklyn and used it to relieve family stress during the war in Kosovo.

The soccer moms attracted media attention, but were stereotyped as women running from the kitchen to the field. Here, Diane Gray enlightens the crew from Lifetime.

Taking on women twenty years younger than her, former rugby player (and mother of teenaged girls) Jeanne Jeffrey was a blur of aggression and elbows.

Ravan Magrath, twenty, was the inexperienced mothers' worst nightmare with her hardheaded play.

Lisa Ciardi's first team, the Bluestone Belles, after winning their first trophies.
Front row, from left: Lisa, Dana DiMuro, Ellen Paretti, Barbara Martoglio.
Back row: Ginger Steuart, Venera Gashi, Jeanne Jeffrey, Beth Albert, Clare Moore.

Beth Fuqua and her son Jeffrey Kerbel at the U.S. Women's World Cup opener at Giants Stadium. Jeffrey brought tears to his mother's eyes by telling her he wanted to be like Mia Hamm, "only a boy."

Beth Albert

Rochelle Sandler

Montclair soccer guru Ashley Hammond and his wife, Meg, honored Lisa at a one-year soccer anniversary party. The women were bitter rivals before Lisa's life took a dramatic turn, one Meg's has already taken.

Vanessa Hardwick

Pokémom Rochelle Sandler joined the soccer moms hoping to fill the companion gap in her life when her daughter left for college.

Robert A. Cummins

The Pokémoms didn't want winning to be their top priority, but any victory was a joyous, albeit rare, occasion.

Wendy Hollender, her hair growing back after cancer treatment, scored a "miracle" hat trick in Ireland to cap her reawakening with the Parlour Moms.

Courtesy of Wendy Hollender

Her experiences as a mother, social worker, and friend taught Barbara Martoglio, center, that soccer symbolized the need to push forward through tough times.

Vanessa Hardwick

Neither the chilly day-long downpour nor the empty stands at Montclair State University dampened spirits for Teamwork 2000, the tournament to raise money for breast cancer programs.

Vanessa Hardwick

Barbara Martoglio (*left*), Dana DiMuro, and Lisa dry out in the locker room between games at the Teamwork 2000 tournament.

Beth Albert

Wendy hands out medals to Lisa's victorious team after the Teamwork 2000 tournament. Inspired, Minnie Evans (*right*) would join Lisa and Venera Gashi in forming their own charity organization, Goals for Life.

Vanessa Hardwick

not need to be coaxed back onto the field; she just needed a name and a telephone number and a pair of cleats that fit.

From all over town and as much as an hour away, Ashley was now getting calls from women, many of them younger, who wanted in. The mothers' party was being crashed, and maybe it was inevitable, because these younger women weren't exactly overwhelmed with recreational choices once they were finished with school. There was no Title IX to govern adults.

As part of the first "younger" wave, Wendy Cogdell was not one to judge the existing talent. For one thing, she hadn't played in several years herself; for another, having recently moved from Texas with her husband, Mike, she was just thrilled to be making new friends. She made one in the Bluestone Belles' Ellen Paretti, with whom she immediately discovered a mutual interest in books. They took to exchanging their favorites as they passed each other coming and going.

Wendy, in fact, had the same reaction to Ravan Magrath and the Badgers as the older women had; she tackled Ravan once, nudging the ball out of bounds. "She was totally freaking out, slamming the ball down, like I had stolen her boyfriend," Wendy said.

One of her new teammates on the Pride, Caroline Quidort, was especially contemptuous of the Badgers. She claimed that one of them—not Ravan—had called her a "dirty bitch" after what she'd considered a fairly routine collision.

Caroline, twenty-three and not long removed from college soccer at a Division I power, the State University at Buffalo, got an eyeful of the older women struggling to keep the ball afoot and thought about how awful it must have been to have grown up without sports. Her mother, now in her early sixties, used to tell her that she'd always wanted to win a trophy; Caroline had boxes full of them back home. Better than that, she had memories, wonderful memories of the tournaments and the games and the trips, when "all you do is play and bond with your team."

But soccer was also about competition, fast and fierce. If Caroline, Wendy, and Jen McEwan—the nucleus of the newly pumped-up Pride—were sympathetic to the older women, they weren't exactly like Camilla Bertelsen; they wanted to play the way they always had. They were perfectly willing to pass the ball to an open mom in the scoring area and to accept the inevitability of a botched shot, but some aspects of this game were nonnegotiable. "I was always telling Lori and our team, 'If you run into somebody or hit somebody, stop saying you're sorry,'" Caroline recalled. "'If you bump somebody, just go on.' There is no such thing as an apology in this game, unless you break someone's leg."

Though it became clear that Beth had only a sprain—which for her was bad enough—Wendy did feel "terrible." She apologized for what the tackle had wrought, if not for the act itself. She thought she'd made a clean play. She had operated within the rules, and in the realm of fair-minded competition. "It's a difficult sport," she said. "There are certain inevitables."

Of course, Beth had another set of inevitables named Jeffrey and Griffin, who were going to wake up the following morning and expect their mother to be the whirlwind of preparation she always was. To make matters worse, Beth's husband, Howard, was leaving that morning on a business trip to London.

When Beth had hurt herself that first day in Brookdale Park, she'd called her brother to brag about her "sports-related injury." That sprain was mild, not inhibiting, yet it raised a red flag: What if she really got hurt? She and Howard discussed her playing such a physical sport, given the demands of motherhood and of his work. "He just said, 'Don't get hurt. Just don't,'" Beth said.

A freak accident was one thing; risking limb, if not life, against women who were almost half her age and trained to play with fire in their eyes was another. Was this what the mothers had bargained for? "No soccer moms are clamoring to learn slide tackling, except maybe Lisa," Beth said.

This was exactly why she wanted the Pokémoms to play in the intermediate league Ashley had created for the second session. It was obvious from the beginning that some of the women were not now and would likely never be ready for the Belles and the Badgers, much less the likes of Caroline and Jen.

The mothers from Livingston had already decided they weren't up for either league; they had thought that everyone in the dome would be a beginner, and they wound up, as Caroline said, "with balls bouncing off their heads." But of the original eight teams, only the Bluestone Belles and Badgers stood out as open league material. Two more teams would be necessary to make the split work. Ashley and Lisa did some prodding and pleading with Beth Fuqua and the Pride's Lori McNamara, and both their teams were given a couple more young players to balance the scales.

Yet for Beth, competitive play for the purpose of winning was still less of a priority than establishing a reasonably safe playing environment. The day after Wendy's slide tackle, she again called her brother, the soccer coach in Virginia. "Dave, tell me if I'm being a baby about this," she said.

He assured her she wasn't. He was thirty years old, playing in an adult league that included some former South American professionals, but also men in their fifties. Slide tackling was not allowed, he said; the fields were in bad condition, with the occasional shard of glass, among other hazards, hidden in the dirt. More important, the probability of injury was much higher when players who had been taught the move properly were matched with those who had not.

"Aren't these former pro players incensed they can't use their full arsenal of weapons?" Beth asked.

"No," he said. "They play hard, but they follow the rules."

Armed with this information, Beth wrote a letter to Ashley, asking why slide tackling and other potentially dangerous tactics were not banned from a league that was still, in certain respects, instructional.

His response was gracious, yet firm: "The move is allowed by FIFA—the soccer governing body of the world. On viewing the games in the dome, it would appear that is a move only a few of the players, both men and women, really wish to attempt. We certainly do not recommend it to anyone who does not know how to successfully master the tackle. At this moment, we do not feel the need to outlaw this move, or anyone who attempts it. Obviously if a foul is committed, then action will be taken, as it would if any other misdemeanor occurred."

In other words, as Ashley said, "slide tackling is an integral part of the game." *Deal with it.*

But there was only so much now that the mothers could deal with, and the Wednesday night intensity alone often seemed too much. The surge of new, younger players had made the Pride a far better team; in the four-team league, almost every game was now competitive and tense, a Belles–Badgers riot about to break out.

Lisa had expanded the Belles' roster to thirteen. She didn't get the best new players, but it was just her luck that Suzanne Kos, a former basketball player, was tall and graceful and had a strong kick. Mary Burke, recruited by Beth Albert from behind the counter at the local Cheese Shop, was another "nonplayer" who was just naturally athletic.

Mary had shown up in Montclair as a frightened but determined eighteen-year-old, looking to escape the depressed job market in Ireland. She was twenty-nine now. Years before, to get a taste of home, she had commuted every weekend to the Bronx to play an Irish game, camogie, with other young immigrant women. She fit right in with the Belles, willing to play any position, even goal, which allowed Sarah Hogan the occasional chance to play up.

The Belles lost their rematch with the Badgers in another tense, one-goal game, and the bad blood between the teams continued to boil. The Belles saw the Badgers as women with chips on their shoulders; the Badgers resented the Belles and blamed them, in part, for turning everyone against them, like meddling sorority sisters. "It was driving us crazy," Ashley said. "After a while, if the Badgers had won the previous week, we'd sit around the office and say, 'I hope they get spanked tonight,'" he said. "And if the Belles had won the previous week, we'd say, 'OK, it's their turn to get spanked.'"

The word choice was unintentional, but then again, the women were acting like schoolgirls—though Ashley could also understand why. "These were wonderful people, wonderful mothers, but completely given over to the passion of soccer, in all the good ways and bad," he said. "It was as if these emotions had been suppressed for twenty years, and some of the women found they couldn't handle them. It became very frenzied, like giving a new drug to people, a strange and new potion. I have power, now what do I do with it?"

Ashley found himself living right in the middle of the cold war between the Badgers and the Belles, between Meg and Lisa. "Lisa is a very competitive lady, but so is my wife," he said. "With the rivalry between the teams, and the way everyone reacted to Ravan and the Badgers, it made Meg defensive, sensitive. She hated Lisa. She'd say, 'She does this, she does that, and all she wants to do is win.' I'd say something in support of Lisa, something to the extent of 'She's really a nice person,' and Meg would just go nuts.

"As a businessman, I was trying to be objective, far more than people would give me credit for. For instance, the women were upset that I didn't show up for intermediate league games, that I only showed up for Meg's games. I was just being a husband, going to see my wife play.

"Even at home it was causing tremendous tension. No matter what I'd say or do, I'd get yelled at. If I gave Meg a hug after the game, I'd get yelled at. If I didn't, I'd get yelled at. I realized that it was difficult for her—she was playing, trying to deal with these emotions, but she was married to me, and it was her business now, too, so she was really right in the middle of it with me."

Most of the husbands were happy that their wives were playing, making priorities of new friends and increased fitness. Yet their support was also being tested by the emotions, the time, and even the money being spent. All of the teams in the open league and several in the intermediate were now practicing on the weekend. Many of the women were playing three times a week, counting the clinics, the practices, and the games.

For some with tighter budgets, the league fees and per clinic costs were not irrelevant. Ellen Paretti said that, as a nonworking mother, she felt guilty constantly asking her husband for money to play soccer. For a few of the younger players, nannies like Camilla and Rilee McDonald, the costs were not insignificant. Yet in an affluent town such as Montclair, the most predictably dramatic effect was the time investment. Soccer was officially cutting into Sunday brunch time, or Sunday *Times* time, or Sunday tee time.

Lisa, for example, made no bones about her irritation when Brian insisted that her soccer was not going to interfere with his weekly golf game. She was, practically speaking, the founder of this group, its acknowledged leader, not to mention her team's captain. How would it look if she couldn't make practice? "There was some tension," she admitted. The solution, most Sundays, was that the kids would come with Lisa, and she would hope some of her teammates would bring along their children for hers to play with.

She wasn't the only one who occasionally found herself leaving the house grumbling, who had to negotiate the "time off"—which was infuriating. How could their husbands not understand what this meant? "The women felt as if they were part of something, part of a movement, an important movement," Ashley said.

In a broader scope, beyond years of habit, it raised a sensitive question: What made a husband's sports and fitness a higher priority than his wife's? Did he deserve more recreational time because, in the formerly conventional setup where he worked and she didn't, he was more entitled after a long week at the office? What about that long week of taking care of the kids, the homework, and the house?

Few spouses could match Mary Sibley's level of productivity. Yet she, too, had to admit that her husband, Jonathan, was sometimes less than enthusiastic about being left at home as she scooted off to practice outdoors. "He'd say, 'When you're at soccer, I've got to watch the kids,'" she reported. Mary didn't want this to become a contentious issue and knew it shouldn't be. Jonathan's own hobby was a Chinese form of yoga and exercise called Qi-gong that required all-day commitments on weekends, and occasional retreats to England and France.

It was clear that for many of these women and their families, behavioral patterns were being changed, ready or not. For a variety of reasons, and from a growing number of sources, passions were running high, often too high. Every Wednesday night, every week, seemed to bring the potential for more upheaval.

What might Ravan do next? Who would get offended or upended? Who was going to take out her frustration, act out of character, and wake up the following morning and think, What the hell did I do? "When we got into the second session, it all got much more competitive all of a sudden, and the women who had not competed in a team sport, particularly a contact sport, seemed to take everything as a personal attack," said Lori McNamara.

As the only girl in a family with four brothers, Lori was practically born into team sports in Vermont. She just never played with girls. She broke the gender barrier in her local Little League. She played football and basketball with her brothers and their friends. She fought and feuded, she said, but when the game was over, everyone went home and forgot everything but the score. "There are always issues in sports, but as a kid you learn to leave it on the field," she said. "There were feelings that the older women had that they weren't able to express right away, so they took it off the field with them, then brought it back. If they thought they got fouled, it became a huge issue, blown way out of proportion. People wouldn't shake hands at the end. There was a lot of nasty, personal talk. Every game, the animosity was getting worse."

Every Wednesday night, the tension level rose a little bit higher. Something or someone in the soccer bubble was bound to burst, and did.

R OCHELLE SANDLER was the first to sense trouble. She had unintentionally sat herself down next to Ravan Magrath while the game between the Pride and the Bluestone Belles was winding down, and the Pokémoms and Badgers were waiting to get on. It was the last night of the second session. Before it was over, the soccer moms would be taking the wildest ride of their short playing careers.

Rochelle, as outgoing as they came and the mother of a teenage girl herself, had talked to Ravan before. Much to her surprise she had found an engaging, self-deprecatingly funny young woman, the complete antithesis of Ravan's on-field persona.

Not this night, though. Not now. Ravan had already acquainted herself with the mathematical ramifications of the season's final games. The defending champion Belles had been eliminated from contention, but they were currently playing the Pride to a draw. If that result held up, then all the Badgers had to do was defeat the Poké-moms, the worst of the four teams, to win the second set of trophies. Anything less than a victory for the Belles meant a title for the Pride.

Ravan was psyched, and Rochelle was spooked. "I was sitting there, and I could see that she was working herself into a frenzy, ranting and raving, saying, 'We have to win, we have to win,'" Rochelle said. Finally, fearing Ravan was going to burst out of her skin before she took to the field, Rochelle decided she had to say something. "Ravan, I'm old enough to be your mother. You can't go out there like that, because you're going to injure somebody, and I don't want to get injured. Now calm down."

"You don't understand," Ravan said. "I hate to lose. I just hate to lose."

Rochelle sighed, and gave up. "Guys, I'm warning you all," she told her teammates after the Belles and the Pride were off the field and the Badgers' must-win scenario was officially in effect. "Watch out for Ravan. She'll do anything to win this game."

Rochelle had already witnessed the results of Beth Fuqua's injury, the weeks of limping around and after her kids. Rochelle needed to be mobile for work, among other things. "I'm telling you all now—I don't care about winning or losing," she said. "If she comes at me, I'm backin' off."

This, unfortunately, was a luxury Nina Sloan didn't have. The slender and intense goalie had nowhere to retreat as the ball rolled toward her early in the game and Ravan bore down. Normally on defense, Ravan was playing up, which made her more of a fury than usual.

"I wanted to score, really wanted to score," she said later. Ravan had already been stopped, head-on in an earlier game, on a direct penalty kick by Nina. It had been a revelatory moment in Nina's short career as a soccer goalie: Not only could she survive, she could thrive.

"I had started seeing this as a lark and fun, and all of a sudden, I'd be up all night, goals going over and over in my head," she said. "For people who had never done that, relative to athletics, that in itself is amazing.

"And then came that penalty kick, against Ravan, and there I am, like, Oh great, of all people. Every time I turned to the left or right, the goal was huge. I knew she had a really strong kick. And she gets up there, and I just totally concentrated on the ball, and I watched—what you do is watch where she looks at the ball, puts her head down, and starts to kick. I didn't guess. I saw what she was doing. It was my right side, my strong side. I leapt at the ball, out of the goal. Somehow I got my hand on it and knocked it away. I beat her on that one. My teammates went crazy. I was in shock. It made me think, I can do this."

On this night, Ravan remembered that Nina was a mom to be reckoned with, which made her run that much harder as the ball rolled toward the goal. It reached Nina before Ravan could get her foot into it. Nina bent down and cradled it with both hands. Ravan slowed to avoid a collision but was unable to veer off. She rolled passively onto Nina, the way one might ease into a cushion.

"She fell into me with her butt, and her legs were wrapped around me," Nina said. "So here's her butt, in my face, and she's not getting off, and my legs are tucked under me and my knees are getting crunched. She's stocky, not light, and she's not getting off."

"Get off me," Nina screamed. "Get . . . *off!*"

Ravan, for her part, said she would have loved to, but the momentum of her run was keeping her down. "If I hadn't stopped myself like that, I would have knocked her over," Ravan said. "That's why I hugged her."

It was only a few seconds, perhaps three or four, but it felt like an eternity to someone who wasn't used to physical confrontation on any sporting level. Nina couldn't breathe, and all the other mothers in the dome held their breath because they intuitively knew this was the moment they had dreaded, the result of weeks of provocation, the inevitable explosion blowing apart that rickety bridge spanning the generation gap.

Just as Beth Fuqua had been "furious" at being slide-tackled, Nina became enraged by Ravan's apparent use of her as an easy chair.

Her right hand instinctively clenched into a fist. And then, before she even consciously understood what she was doing, she was using it, pummeling Ravan's back.

The referee, Darryl Billington, raced over to pull them apart. Ravan was up. Nina jumped up. Ravan immediately saw the cards coming out of Darryl's pocket—a red and a yellow. "Don't red-card me," she screamed. "Don't red-card me!"

Nina, oblivious to the difference between a red card, a yellow card, or, for that matter, a green card, was still in shock. "She wouldn't get off. I just wanted her off," she shouted to Darryl.

Ravan got a yellow card, the warning. "OK," she said, calming down. "That's OK."

Nina was red-carded, ejected from this game and whenever her team might play the next one. Ejected? She didn't understand. Her? As if returning to consciousness, Nina couldn't believe what she was hearing. "She sat on me and I'm out of the game?"

Darryl tried to explain to her that it had been automatic the second she lifted a hand.

"Then why aren't we both out?" Nina demanded.

Darryl said that, in his opinion, Ravan had been entitled to go for the ball, and had not deliberately run into her. It was a strict interpretation of the rules, but Nina, bringing a different kind of logic, couldn't believe the provocateur—Ravan, of all people—could stay in the game.

Her teammates tried to console her, but Nina left the field hopping mad. She tried to engage Ashley, who waved her off, saying this wasn't the time or place. The referee had to be in control; his call was final. She could watch the remainder of the game from the sideline, but she was out.

"I felt terrible for Nina, the thought of her being driven to that kind of violence," Rochelle said. "And I thought, Look what our little fun experience has become, a competitive brawl. Is this what it's about?"

To make it worse, there was still a game to be played, and the Pokémoms would now have to play six against seven, with their roster already depleted and short of subs. As if they hadn't been playing with enough of a talent disadvantage from the start. The dome, its tight sideline area jammed with the players from the Pride and the Belles and various family members, was now in an uproar. As the game resumed, Mike Cogdell—Wendy's husband and one of the Pride's most vociferous fans—began yelling for someone to "take Ravan out, take her out." Even in their aroused and victimized state, the Pokémoms looked over at him as if he were mad. Wendy ordered him to calm down immediately.

Lori McNamara was cringing at the thought that her son, Casey, was watching the spectacle along with her, but she couldn't walk out on the Pokémoms now. She had to stay, given the remote possibility that the Pokémoms could win or tie. Her team then stood to win the championship trophies.

The Pokémoms were obviously bewildered by the bizarre turn of events, but within minutes it became apparent that they were playing harder. Faster. And against all expectations and odds, better than they ever had. Could it have been the tide of sentiment? The collective emotions that had been spraying in all directions but were now focused on a singular assignment: Keep the Badgers from winning this game, from getting the trophies?

"We wanted the Pride to win, no question, and we didn't want to see the Badgers win," said Lisa, head of the Belles' cheering contingent. "This was all just an accumulation of everything that had happened."

The Badgers scored a goal to go ahead, but the Pokémoms tied the score when Meg, playing defense, accidentally knocked one in for an own goal.

The game went into the second half. Camilla, having replaced Nina in goal, got caught up in the frenzy and threw her body around like a human shield. With every save, with every passing minute, the dome got louder, Lori and Jen McEwan and the other Pride players joining in a rowdy chorus with the Bluestone Belles.

None of the mothers on the field—or on the sideline, for that matter—had ever experienced anything quite like this. Beth Panucci was so energized, so frenzied, that she continually hurtled herself in the direction of the ball, falling repeatedly, until Meg, her opponent, suggested she calm down or she was going to get hurt.

Even Rochelle told herself, To hell with caution, fear, and Ravan: We can do this. "We played our hearts out," she said.

Donna Farrell lined up a penalty shot with just a few minutes remaining and the score still 1–1. Donna, a thirty-year-old sports photographer and graphics designer, was one of the few experienced Pokémoms players. Her kick could have put a Badgers victory out of reach. But she missed, and the Badgers controlled the play, pressing for the one goal they needed, only to be denied by Camilla time after time. "She was unbelievable," Nina said, "like she had this natural connection to the ball."

Back on the sideline, Mike Cogdell was keeping unofficial time on his stopwatch. According to his calculation, it appeared the game was being extended beyond regulation. "They're not going to stop it until the Badgers score," he told Wendy, the Ashley-Meg conspiracy theory alive and well. Wendy had to talk him out of confronting Ashley then and there.

Suddenly Darryl Billington was blowing his whistle, waving off play. Tie game. Championship to the Pride. The Pride and Belles spilled onto the field to congratulate the somewhat dazed Pokémoms. The Badgers couldn't believe they hadn't won, and how badly all these people hadn't wanted them to.

The trophies were awarded. Then Donna Farrell, still upset she had missed the penalty kick that could have won the game for the Pokémoms, decided she needed to practice. Let it go, said the older Pokémoms, thrilled with the tie. Even Nina, temporarily suspending her personal horror, was going out to party. The tumultuous first year of playing for keeps was over. Summer and soccer league vacation were upon them. It was time for everyone to celebrate, to drink as one.

"Tierney's!" someone called out.

Except for the Badgers, of course. Still trophy-less and seemingly more isolated than ever, they retreated sadly to their hangout in West Orange. And Ravan, with no more soccer games to lose herself in, with only the reality of her mother's terminal illness, broke down in tears.

9

Breaking Up Is Hard to Do

THE AUGUST MORNING was sunny, breezy, near perfection in the park. Lisa Ciardi strolled across the expanse of grass parched by drought and found a seat under a small tree that only partially obscured the light. From all around came the sounds of soccer, which were music to Lisa's ears, the dozens of kids churning through another session of Ashley's Soccer Camp. Squinting against the sun, she searched far and wide for a glimpse of her own.

A year had elapsed since that first contact with Steve Cook, and here she was, still waiting for the kids to finish up, but with her own water bottle by her side, happily fatigued after her own two-hour workout. Imagine that! After too many years of standing off to the side, Lisa was a camper now, too.

The soccer moms' group that was now an Ashley's Soccer Camp feature adjourned an hour before the kids, and Lisa enjoyed being in the park, stretching out her stressed muscles, sneaking peeks at John and the girls. Then she would settle under a tree and contemplate the day, but with a far healthier perspective than in the past. She was no longer the mere shepherd of her children. Her days began as theirs did now: They strapped on their shin guards together, slipped into their cleats, rushed through their breakfast. Lisa was a year older, but she felt so much younger, more alive, the way she had as that Brooklyn tomboy who loved playing football in the narrow street.

The kids, especially John, loved being at camp every morning, week after week, and Lisa was not about to argue with them. She would drop them at the curb, see them off to their respective groups, then park the car and jog across the grass to meet up with the other mothers in her group. Some of them were Badgers, but even that block of ice had begun to melt under the hot summer sun.

"This is ridiculous, we're all mothers, why are we acting this way?" Minnie Evans, the Badgers' goalie, had blurted out after one typically frosty session. Nobody could think of a sensible answer, so Lisa and Meg and several of their respective teammates left together and broke breakfast bread. The war wasn't completely over; there always seemed to be a new hot-button issue. Someone still got "bent out of shape," as Lisa put it, every time the women stepped inside the dome for a Wednesday night pay 'n' play. The Badgers would want to compete together. The other women would claim the competition was supposed to be strictly choose-up. Why should they serve as practice dummies for the Badgers and make them stronger for the fall?

One night Caroline Quidort got into an argument with Meg and stormed off, announcing—prematurely, as it turned out—she wasn't coming back.

It finally reached the point where Ashley threatened, with his fingers crossed behind his back, to throw the women out. Jeanne Jeffrey was convinced that he would, that the women would not make it to the next September league. She took it upon herself to write

Ashley a letter to thank him for the effort and to say how much the experience had meant to her. He posted the letter on a wall in the office so he and his staff could calm themselves the next time someone complained.

"It was something about the dome that set things off, like it was an arena that brought out the anger in people," Jeanne said. It was much calmer in the park, as if nature itself was anesthesia for the ego.

In June, Lisa and Lori McNamara had procured a permit for a field in Brookdale Park and created yet another soccer vehicle, a Monday evening free-for-all. There was no league, no refs, no set teams, no score kept. If thirty women showed up, there would be fifteen players a side, playing all at once. Under such unsanctioned, unstructured conditions, the mothers became less wary about skill levels, about making mistakes. As the summer drought wreaked havoc with the field, they usually wound up a dusty, giddy mess.

"Very free, play wherever you want," Lisa said. "There were kids running around on the side, dogs breaking loose, the day cooling down, the sun setting. It relieved a lot of the stress people felt at the dome."

It made it easier for the generations to communicate, to compete, to coexist. One Monday night Beth Fuqua found herself walking off with Jen McEwan. "You looked good tonight," Jen said.

"When you first started, you sucked, but now you don't suck" was what Beth made of Jen's casual tribute. She knew she was reading too much into it, as the mothers tended to do, yet she couldn't stop herself. She was grateful nonetheless.

Beth also recognized that she had something to offer Jen and Camilla and Caroline. "I'm hoping the younger players are learning that when you're thirty-eight like me, or forty-five, you can try things totally new," Beth said. "A friend of mine started cello lessons. Cello. Soccer. Whatever."

Whatever had gone on and was yet to come, this summer was

magic for so many of them, beginning with a galvanizing outing to Giants Stadium in July for the opening ceremonies and games of the Women's World Cup. It seemed as if half of Soccer Moms Montclair were there, scattered in bunches in the lower stand. Lisa sat with her teammates Dana and Clare and Venera, who absolutely freaked when she realized the great Pelé was pressing the flesh just a few rows behind them. Venera rushed up to get his autograph; her brothers, her whole extended family on two continents, would have given her hell if she hadn't.

The women on the field—Mia and Brandi, Julie and Kristine—were the real role models, though, and Lisa knew she could appreciate this celebration in a way that would not have been possible were she not a soccer player herself.

They all watched the final victory over China from the Rose Bowl in Pasadena together at one of the local bars. By the time the penalty kicks were up, it was bedlam. It was heaven. Let's face it, Lisa thought as they celebrated the U.S. victory, her timing could not have been better. She had lit the soccer moms' fuse at the perfect moment for an American female to be part of this particular sport. Growing pains aside, the feeling she had when women came up and thanked her—a fairly common occurrence these days—was almost indescribable. "Not that I expected it," Lisa said, "but it is special to hear that putting all this together has meant something to so many women who are really happy to be here."

A few weeks earlier Lisa and the core mothers, in full camp regalia, had clomped onto Venera's patio to say thank you to another deserving soul. Steve Cook was leaving for a job at one of his previous stops, in Troy, Michigan. While the burgers grilled, while they all reminisced about the early days and Steve and Dave Law complained about their excessive chatter during those first drills, the mothers took turns sneaking into the kitchen to sign one of the T-shirts currently on sale at Soccer Domain.

SOCCER MOMS—BORN TO PLAY, it read across the front.

Lisa presented it to Steve, who slipped it over his head. Champagne glasses were filled. Ellen Paretti raised her glass and offered a heartfelt toast. "You changed our lives," she said.

Ellen could not have said it better, as far as Lisa was concerned. Over the previous months she had come to feel so different, so much surer about herself. The very term "soccer mom" was heard in a completely different and far more positive context. She was certain her children had had their own perspectives altered, and that alone would have made it all worthwhile.

The kids understood now that when Lisa had a game or a practice and Dad wasn't home, they had to go with her. John, about to start fourth grade and getting to the point where he could dribble rings around the soccer moms and dads, gave her tips. Olivia always wanted to play with Lisa. Even Madeline, weeks away from kindergarten, who had often cried the previous spring when Lisa would get ready to leave for a game at night, had caught the fever. "Mommy, are you playing China?" she asked one night when Lisa was almost out the door.

More and more Lisa enjoyed speaking the same language as the rest of her family. When she talked about soccer, about players and games, she used expressions like "step up" and "next level." Sounds and sights were not deceiving—a woman who once typically wore long, flowery dresses could now be seen rushing around town in the uniform of the uncompromising jock: soccer shorts or knee-high tights, with the occasional wrap around the elbow or knee.

She wanted to hold on to these long summer days that began in camp and often ended over a beer with her new friends, who seemed to be evolving into her closest friends. She wanted to lock into her newfound state of aggression, to push herself harder.

Not every mother felt the way she did, Lisa knew. As the months went by she could sense the widening divide, the shifting levels of ambition and skill. Many of the other mothers, several on her own team, were already knee-deep in doubt about whether to remain in the open league come September or to drop down a notch to the intermediate level.

There were artists and designers, musicians and teachers in this crowd. Every time Cathy Wright threw up her hand when she took a turn in goal so Nina Sloan could play afield, she was, in effect, risking her livelihood. They had all seen what happened to Beth Fuqua when she was slide-tackled. Did it make sense for them to risk injury against younger women? Did they want to feel insecure about their skills, or to sit on the bench and become, in large part, cheerleaders in cleats?

Distribution of minutes had inevitably become an issue on all four teams in the open league during the spring schedule. Once the younger, experienced players came aboard and the rosters grew, playing time in the tense, competitive games began to be awarded on merit. In the first go-round Lisa had made the substitutions for the Bluestone Belles, not a terribly difficult chore when there were fewer players and the Belles were winning their games easily, with the exception of the most important one, against the Badgers.

The second league was something else entirely. For one thing, Karen Sherris was their official coach now, and, not counting the injured Ginger Steuart, Lisa had twelve players on the roster. Most nights Karen had five substitutes for what was only a forty-minute game, soon to be expanded to fifty.

As the games became closer, the atmosphere became more demanding. Players like Ellen Paretti and Barbara Martoglio found themselves on the sideline, the minutes flying by in the second half, with the sudden and demoralizing realization that they probably weren't going back in. "I don't like what's happening, the way this is working out," Barbara had said one night, clearly stressed, as the Belles furiously tried to make up a one-goal deficit against the Pride and the substitution rotation was unceremoniously scrapped.

"Barbara, calm down," said Dana, standing alongside her. "It's not that important."

Even Barbara's husband tried to steer her to that logical conclusion after she went home that night feeling personally defeated. "If you're going to be sad about this, move on, move down, or to another team," Ed said.

But that was the catch: You couldn't invest this much energy, this much time, away from your family and your other recreational interests, and then compare it to switching checkout lines in the supermarket. In their original form, only weeks earlier, the Bluestone Belles had more than excelled; they had established what Barbara and the others had thought was a special bond. There was a reason why, for Barbara, the team photo had meant so much more than the championship trophy. And now those same women were sending her and a couple of the others a subliminal but most deflating message: Get lost.

"It shot my self-esteem at first, creating a whole process of soul-searching," Barbara admitted. "Do I want to continue feeling nervous before a game and feel even worse after a game? It would have been nice to have had a team meeting and have everyone talk about it, but then part of me was afraid the answer would be 'Well, you're not good enough.'"

When the season was over she instead talked to Lisa, whose leadership and sensitivity she trusted. Lisa admittedly felt herself pinned between a rock and a hard place, between loyalty to her friends and her own emerging competitive needs. "I realized some of the women weren't getting much game time," she said. "That bothered me. But I also felt we wanted to win."

She knew that Jeanne and Venera and Clare and, of course, Sarah in goal felt as she did, wanting to compete at the highest possible level. To play to win. She also intuitively understood that a player ultimately had to be realistic about her ability. They were not children being guided by youth coaches. They had to figure out for themselves when to go forward, when to step back. Some weekend golfers clung to fantasies about playing the senior tour someday. Others could just enjoy a good walk spoiled. Sports, like anything else, was about finding your level, your place, as long as those options existed.

This was one of those conditioned tenets of team sports that a Caroline or a Jen or a Ravan would presumably have had less trouble accepting. Kids' teammates changed season to season; some moved on to the more advanced levels, to travel teams, and some didn't. Some dropped out. Every year brought a new team with a modified or completely restructured dynamic. Steve Cook told Lisa that changing teams on the basis of ability was part of the learning process that he and his mates had grappled with when they were lads; it wasn't easy, but eventually you learned it was part of the game.

Like swimming, this was harder to learn as an adult. Lisa recognized that Barbara and Ellen and Beth Albert and one or two of the others were waiting for her, as the team leader and spokeswoman, to participate in their decisions. She couldn't, though. They had to draw their own conclusions, which Barbara was the first to do. "In retrospect, I really knew," she said. "I mean, I really didn't need to talk to anybody about it. It's your own feelings and doing what was right for you. You really couldn't expect your friends to say, 'We don't think you're good enough.'"

Of course, Barbara had the benefit of teenage team sports. She could decide to play in the less competitive league and still look up at the Belles' photo in her living room and feel good about the experience. Ellen, by contrast, had nothing else to draw on; for her the experience was like being jilted by her first love. She found herself wanting from Lisa the cold, hard truth, a more official severance, as if her withdrawal from the Belles was also a commentary on the state of their friendships. The hurt lingered. She began to feel that since she had been injured for part of the first season and wasn't one of the better players, she didn't really belong in that championship photo. She removed it from a display on the main floor of her home. She took the trophy and handed it to her youngest son, Ben, who had wanted one to match that of his big brother, David, the kinder kicker. "I thought, Don't make yourself feel part of that team because you weren't at the time and you're not anymore," she said.

Ellen then offered to surrender her Belles jersey to Lisa. "Keep it," Lisa said, adding that she and Clare and the others had decided to change the team color and name.

This news only made Ellen's wounds deeper. "I guess they really want to disassociate themselves from us," she told Barbara.

"I never looked at it that way," Barbara said. "I thought, They want to remember that team the way it was, the team that won the trophy, that took the picture." And that, Lisa and Clare both said, was exactly why they'd decided to retire the Bluestone Belles. It was more out of respect for Ellen and Barbara and Beth, for their sharing in something that would always be unique.

By late August, Lisa still had not thought of another name. She entered her team for the September open league as Team X.

None of the other teams had even submitted rosters by the deadline Ashley imposed. This created another row, over the recruitment of new players. Lori McNamara said it was her understanding that the league would incorporate incoming players and distribute them fairly, based on ability. She claimed that the Badgers were scouting and stocking their roster, and that Ashley was turning the other cheek in deference to Meg.

Ashley responded that the league could not possibly control adult player personnel in the way it did with the youth teams, if only because the captains hadn't even entered their teams. As a result, he had decided to let them organize the rosters on their own. In other words, it was open season for recruiting younger players.

"We're mothers, how are we supposed to find new players?" Lori asked. After a raucous meeting in which she felt unsupported by the other women and under attack, Lori announced she'd had enough, and quit.

Meg, meanwhile, was still disturbed by all the unrestrained emotions, including her own. The Badgers had experienced the same playing-time issues as the Belles, and Meg did not enjoy seeing some of her players afraid to go back in the game after their teammates on the sideline had yelled at them to sub out. She couldn't sleep for three nights after she, too, got carried away in one of the heated summer games in the dome and found herself hunting a woman on the other team, practically looking for a fight. "I just wanted to be anonymous, to just play, but I couldn't," she said.

Tired of being cast alternately as Ashley's beneficiary and as a Badger villainess, she decided she was better off retiring for the time being and moving into the front office. She could get the exercise she needed to keep her right-side muscles strong at the various soccer mom clinics.

Back in the park, however, the Monday night game just kept growing, as women from all over the area learned of the happenings in Montclair. Every week it seemed as if there were four or five faces no one had seen before. Walking off one night with Beth Fuqua, Dana said, "I didn't know who half these women were." Nobody, least of all the original soccer moms, seemed to know how many more were coming and where they were all going. It was understandably scary in some respects. Threatening. Not for Lisa, though. She thought that the unknown competitive challenge was the fun and the point of it all.

•   •   •

O N T H E E V E N I N G in the park that the father went nuts, the women's weekly game on the adjacent field came to a sudden and screeching halt. They all stood and watched in utter disbelief. The father, who was not coaching, apparently had some kind of beef with the referee and proceeded to make the worst kind of youth-sports spectacle of himself. Ranting. Raving. Posturing. Cursing. On the other field the mothers could only imagine which of the kids was the one being shamed. "Nice role model," one of the women finally yelled out in a moment of calm, and everyone froze, half-expecting the lunatic to turn on them.

Beth Fuqua left that scene fairly horrified, wondering: Is that what sports must invariably become? A fragile coexistence someone was ready to obliterate over an offside call?

This very issue had been on her mind over the previous weeks as she contemplated her six-year-old's entry into youth league soccer in the town's first-grade league, as well as her own continued involvement following her injury from the collision with Wendy Cogdell. And then she came upon an article on the Sunday op-ed page of *The New York Times* that made such an impression on her she clipped and saved it. The piece, headlined WE CAN'T ALL WIN THE WORLD CUP, was written by Cynthia Gorney, an associate professor of journalism at the University of California at Berkeley.

Within the text were two cartoons—one of several girls in soccer uniforms celebrating, and another of one girl, sitting on a ball, lonely and sad. While the author had celebrated the World Cup final like millions of other American women turned breathless by the event, she was also left with a troubling notion—what if the Chinese women had won the Cup? Would the American women have woken up to a yawning indifference the next day? Did women have to win, did they have to be great, to get the attention and acclaim, or even equal access to the field? "It's the way we do organized sports in this country," she wrote. "*Better* and *more competitive* are synonymous. It's the guy model. It's venerable. It seems to be the only way we have."

Cynthia had coached her own daughter's youth soccer teams and experienced the joy of watching girls who were surely not going to play Olympic or even travel soccer but had learned to overcome simple fears—of collisions, of the ball, of even setting foot on a field. It was thrilling to watch them develop a sense of belonging, the presumption of participation even if they weren't aiming for the stars. But she also noticed that when her daughter eventually moved on to a travel team, there were no more woman coaches, and not nearly as much of what she called "the giggles," or plain fun. In her *Times* article Cynthia warned against women getting "too caught up in the heroics of competition and World Cup," lest we "spend so much time celebrating the ascension of great athletes that we stop paying attention to the girls who only want to get out there and play."

She spoke from her own soccer-playing experiences, from what she called "My Life as a Late-Blooming Jock." And hers had begun just the way it had for Lisa Ciardi and Beth Fuqua: a bunch of Bay Area mothers who several years before, standing around watching their little ones have all the fun, had decided, What the hell, let's give it a shot.

Cynthia wound up on an over-thirty coed team and had so much to say on the subject that she had occasionally given thought to writing a book. "Coed turned out to be complicated," she wrote in one E-mail dispatch, expanding on her op-ed piece, in lieu of an interview.

> There was definitely flirting involved, although most of us were happily married. It was more flirting of the eight-year-old puppies-in-the-mud nature. I loved it for a whole load of reasons. It was loud. It was outdoors. It involved flinging my body into people and trying to run faster than they did.

I had so little experience with physical teamwork that this, too, was a revelation, the almost sexual thrill of the successful assist. On our team, the men passed to the women most of the time, sometimes not enough when the pressure was on, but I didn't actually mind that. They were, in fact, better, and they seemed to be playing coed for the same reasons we were. Nothing to prove in quite the same way as the men's game.

It was fun; I can't say that emphatically enough. It made me realize how many of us lead grown-up lives short of what we used to define as fun when we were kids. At our games, we shrieked at each other, poured water on each other's heads, shouted private jokes, yelled things in code.

When I played, there was a sort of electroshock effect, two hours of concentrating on a small, white spherical object, no time left over for obsessing on matters of work or marriage. After the Thursday night practices, I got in the bathtub and then watched *ER* and stretched my sore shoulders and thought: Bliss. Small moment of perfect and utterly self-absorbed happiness, the thing so famously elusive in the conventional mom-wife-working-woman mode. A life generally quite wonderful but ripped into fragments in the customary modern manner.

In our league, which was called the Old Saturday Stumblers, we started in the D Division (the lowest), worked our way up to B, and then, after I blew out my knee, the team settled back into C, where it now seems to be happily residing.

Residing. It was an interesting word choice, giving the impression that Cynthia wasn't trying to get anywhere, other than to the other side of the field with the ball. She just wanted to keep running and laughing and stretching out those sore shoulders afterward. When her daughter eventually left for the travel team, Cynthia continued coaching the "regular girls like me, who don't want to drop into the big merit sieve of American sports."

But she concluded in her *Times* piece, "No, I haven't worked out a wondrous alternative system that gives equal push and enthusiasm to both the Brandi Chastains and the ordinary girls who can't run very fast."

Back in Montclair, Beth Fuqua finished Cynthia's article convinced she needed a more comfortable, secure place to reside if she was going to continue playing. She recognized that she was one of those girls Cynthia had been talking about. She didn't want to quit because she'd been hurt.

Her resolve to continue—albeit on her own terms—was heightened by the World Cup, on her date with her six-year-old at the moment when he asked if he could have a Mia Hamm jersey. Jeffrey changed his mind by the time they were near the front of the concession line, but with an acknowledgment that still brought tears to Beth's eyes. "When I grow up," he said, "I want to be like Mia, but a boy."

There were too many rewards that outweighed the risks, Beth realized. At least there was now a place in the dome for the "regular girls." That's where Beth decided she was going. The Pokémoms did not belong in a slide-tackle, cutthroat league. If Beth had become captain by default, well, she was the captain. And, after consulting with the others, she was making the decision to move her team down. Those younger players who wanted to stay could form their own team.

Beth also invited the breakaway Bluestone Belles—Ellen Paretti, Barbara Martoglio, and Beth Albert—to join her team. She welcomed them and the remaining Pokémoms to a meeting at which she introduced the players one by one, articulating the positives each would bring. She passed out agenda sheets, precipitating a discussion of team issues:

- Level of training (frequency of practice, with or without coach)
- Coach candidates
- Positions (people's preferences, rotate or specialize, goalkeeper)
- Substitution during games (individually or as a line, and how often)
- Balancing (desire to win, playing time, and learning through experience)

By the end of the meeting it was clear that the Pokémoms had a clear consensus: no yelling, have fun, play hard, stay sane. They agreed it would be helpful to have a coach, if only to organize them and keep track of the substitutions. Beth Albert said she would approach Filip Bondy, a sports columnist for the New York *Daily News,* a Montclair resident, family friend, and longtime soccer devotee whose children were now too old for him to coach.

There was only one issue left unresolved: Who could, or would, play goalie?

Rochelle suggested they ask Nina Sloan, though they all had been under the impression that Nina was going to remain in the open league. After only a few months at the position, Nina was already one of the two or three best goalies in the league. The young players made it clear they wanted her to stay up. But there were those emotional scars from her debacle with Ravan.

They hadn't faded. Months later, sitting in her living room, Nina could still recall the postfight hours, getting home from the three-team celebration at Tierney's between eleven and midnight. Alternately sobbing and raging, she wrote a long letter to Ashley, finishing at 2:00 A.M. They spoke on the phone the next day for more than an hour. Ashley said he would be happy to respond to her letter, but rules were rules, and in his league the ref's ruling was final. "I agree to disagree with you," she told him. "No hard feelings."

She never sent the letter. What was done was done. It was the aftermath that scared her. "What that incident brought about was a real uprising in the ways that women can play this sport in this town," she said. "It may have been at my expense. But there are a lot of women who have decided that they don't want to play that way. They're not doing this to be that competitive, and it caused a lot of women to say, 'Hey, we don't need that level. We just want to do this to have fun.'"

They had all been more than supportive of her that night at Tierney's, but she had known most of them only a few months. What must they really be thinking? she worried. "That I am capable of trying to beat somebody up?" she asked. "In my heart, all I walked away with was embarrassment. I was mortified. More important than tieing that game, what were these people going to think of me in my own community? That I'm like some animal?"

At least her seven-year-old son, Sam, hadn't been there to see it. That was one consolation. But it didn't help the following morning when she went to the supermarket and bumped into one of the Belles, who smiled mischievously and said, "Well, don't you have a violent streak?"

Nina wasn't naming names, and she conceded it was likely just a lighthearted greeting following a wild and crazy night. Yet in her stressed state at the time, she took it as something much worse. "It confirmed my worst fears," she said. It told her that people were still talking about it, about her. Before summer, before they all scattered, she knew she had to set the record straight in some way. Nina took herself to one of the morning clinics in the park, and she went out for breakfast afterward with some of the others. "I was able to tell my story, that I had a motivation for doing this," she said. "And it all came out."

For Nina that was the last of soccer for the summer. She couldn't bring herself to go to the Monday night game in the park, and certainly not back to the dome. "That whole incident made me step back and say, 'What am I doing here?'" she said. What did she want out of this game?

After the Pokémoms' meeting, Rochelle kept after her to move down—at temple, at the opening fall practices for their boys' travel teams. Beth Fuqua left a message on her answering machine. Nina had to admit that the pure and competitive athlete in her wanted to go ahead and compete with the better players. But the forty-one-year-old working mother was asking, "What, exactly, are you trying to prove?"

That part of her was drawing the same conclusion that Cynthia Gorney and so many others around the country had come to: They didn't have to use the guy model. They could make sports whatever they wanted sports to be. They had every right to kick, pass, and throw like a girl.

10

MOB Rule

WHILE MANY OF THE Montclair women were facing a metaphorical soccer crossroads, Cindy Aserkoff was hitting an actual road back to when the only blow she could strike for women's sports came during color war. Not that Cindy was any great athlete deprived of personal fortune and fame. She just always enjoyed sports, considered herself "decent," and wished she had the same kinds of childhood memories the boys she knew could carry with them into middle age.

"Shining moments," Cindy called them, but the sad truth all these years later was that she could think of only one, that glorious day at sleep-away camp in Allentown, Pennsylvania, when she heroically served out the volleyball match. "I was about fourteen," she said. "It was color war, so everybody got to play. I must have served the last ten or twelve points."

It wasn't the score that mattered all these years later, it was the opportunity, the experience, the memory. It was the notch on the belt that tightens self-esteem. Above all what Cindy remembered about that day was that it was just a damn good time.

And that was why, at fifty, Cindy had for almost a decade juggled her family time and her work as a project manager in the computer industry with the bureaucratic blizzard of effort required to run an over-thirty women's basketball league out of Fairfax, Virginia. That, and her latest innovation and departure from convention.

Camp AWOL, Cindy had named her late-summer weekend get-away the previous August, when she practically dared her friends to post a note on the refrigerator with the camp address, phone number, and explanation of the acronym: Athletic Women on Leave. Almost fifty women took her up on the challenge, so here she was, ready and raring to go AWOL again.

Cindy's own girls had once been campers at Timber Ridge, 750 rustic acres nestled in the foothills of the Shenandoah Mountains in West Virginia. But Cory was in college now, and Jodi was a high school soccer player; it was Cindy's turn to be a camper again.

Most of the women were from the D.C. area, from her basketball league, but there were a few from New York and New Jersey, and Nora Silver was coming all the way from outside Berkeley, California. Cindy and Nora were childhood friends, camp bunkmates, who were still close enough to vacation together when they hit a milestone birthday every five years.

Timber Ridge wasn't exactly Cancún, to which Cindy and Nora had just months ago escaped for the Big Five-O. That was personal; Camp AWOL was more along the lines of athletic group therapy. For the paltry sum of fifty dollars—less than it cost Cindy and her friends for a good seat and two hours of vicarious WNBA thrills in downtown D.C.—they could make their own excitement. Choose a sport, pick your passion, go for a swim, nap under a tree, apply an icy beer bottle to that inevitable bruised elbow or knee.

Have a ball. That was Cindy's daylong mantra, and all she asked was that you not get carried away with the desire to win, not whine about the calls, and if you must keep score, then do everyone a favor and keep it to yourself.

Cindy was like that lonely little girl in the cartoon alongside Cynthia Gorney's *New York Times* op-ed piece, now all grown up and firm in the conviction that it was perfectly all right to participate in sports in her own depressurized way. Take the game-winning shot out, the postgame agony of defeat away, the edge off, and what have you got? "A niche," Cindy said. "I have a niche."

A decade earlier, when Cindy was forty and her girls were elementary school age, it was more like an itch, the same temptation that had propelled Lisa Ciardi across that invisible line in Brookdale Park. In fact, Cindy and her friends had started out just like the women in Montclair, kicking a soccer ball and mimicking their children, a summer fancy that included a trip to instructional camp.

"They had us doing 'duck duck goose,' all this stuff, and we had a good time as long as we were playing with women our own age," she said. "But we had an experience one time where there were two fields, an over-thirty group and an under-thirty group, and, for whatever reason, there weren't enough women in the under-thirty group so they wound up playing in our game. I couldn't run up and down the field with them, and, plus, they had attitudes and weren't very kind. I said, 'That's it.'"

She quit soccer. She thought about giving up her brief sports fling altogether, giving in to the realization that the young women were too strong, too aggressive, too intimidating, and much too plentiful. She conceded that the daughters of Title IX—like the girls in her own house—were inheriting the fields, and the last place she wanted to be was in their way.

Then it occurred to her that she didn't need to play soccer, nor did she need a whole field. Her favorite sport had always been basketball, be it NBA, NCAA, or the terrific girls' high school teams that packed a few thousand fans into gymnasiums all over northern Virginia. Cindy wasn't tall and couldn't jump and barely knew how to shoot. She nonetheless proceeded to organize a couple dozen women from soccer and work, and the next thing she knew they were camped out in a tiny elementary school gymnasium with a strange carpetlike floor that gave them all rug burns from tripping over basketballs and their own two feet.

"We were just pathetic," Cindy said. "A lot of us didn't know the rules, weren't very athletic, but it was such an easy thing to come and play, and so unthreatening, that we were all comfortable."

Cindy handpicked a couple of evenly balanced teams. Her husband, Robert, a Sunday morning pickup player, was supportive from the start and agreed to ref. And they all decided, in the spirit of maintaining their comfort zone, that keeping score was a burden they neither wanted nor needed.

They just played, and it was such a liberating experience, their own collective statement, that almost a decade later the Mothers of Basketball (MOB) were still playing with scoreboard zeros as frozen in place as fossils. Cindy's niche caught on. The league grew and was now operating in some form almost year-round. There was an advanced league for those younger over-thirty players, the "post IXers," who were showing up in greater numbers every year. Cindy was at the point where she had to keep a waiting list of aspiring players.

And still, as if celebrating their main point, as if settling an old score, Cindy and her Mothers of Basketball refused to keep it.

•   •   •

THE JEWISH COMMUNITY CENTER was a short drive from Cindy's home in an upper-middle-class Fairfax neighborhood of winding streets that were ghostly quiet on a winter's Sunday evening. She was anxious to get to the gym this night, the regular game night, because she had been away the previous week, and, naturally, an issue had come up that required her attention. "A situation in the advanced league," she said.

It was the first thing her husband mentioned when he'd picked her up at the airport as she returned from her trip to Cancún with Nora the previous Sunday. "There's a woman who took another player out," Robert said, having come straight from the gym. "Claire went up for a ball and got her legs cut out from underneath."

Cindy knew exactly who the culprit was. She had already noticed this woman, new to the league, playing a little too aggressively. "I'm going to watch her tonight," Cindy said. "If I see one thing, I'll pull her off and say, 'We don't play like that. You need to find another place to play.'"

Cindy had done it before. She would do it again. There were other basketball leagues in the area where women could box out, take a charge, play as passionately and physically as Pat Summitt would demand. Not in Cindy Aserkoff's leagues, though. Not with this MOB.

"I'm basically a control freak, and I've always wanted to make sure the leagues stayed exactly as they were," Cindy said. "I assign the teams, always have. You fill out the form and put down beginner, intermediate, or advanced, and I'll put 'em where they say they belong. Some will put down intermediate, but I'll see them and think they're advanced; I'll go up to them after the first night and say, 'You need to play in the advanced.'

"I also reserve the right to split up a team. I've got an issue with one right now. Too many skilled players. They knew it, but they were sending me E-mails before this season, saying they car-pool, they go out to eat. I told them, 'I'm going to have to force you to split up.' Even though we don't keep score, you know when you're getting killed."

And that was never the point of Cindy's leagues, though more than a few women had tried over the years to convince her that it was all right to keep score, that sports was merely a reflection of life, a competition in itself that was inevitably measured by victory and defeat. "What makes you think we're not competitive just because we don't keep score?" Cindy would say.

Her friend Susan Crawford argued that the purpose of recreational team sports was not—or shouldn't be anyway—to build up one's ego by deflating someone else's. In her professional life conducting business seminars, she knew there had been a dramatic operational shift in the previous decade: Teamwork had become the essence of corporate competition. Susan believed that the long struggle for precious opportunity in the workplace, along with a lack of exposure to teamwork as children, had made many women more competitive with each other than cooperative. As far as she was concerned, everything positive she needed from sports she could get playing Cindy's way.

Tall, broad-shouldered, and blond, Susan looked very much like a serious athlete and probably would have been one if she were twenty-five years younger. Her son was a college football player. At fifty she often surprised younger women when she told them she was "only a cheerleader" in college at Wake Forest. "I always thought of myself as a nonathlete, and my teammates couldn't depend on me," she said. "But what's been great is developing the feeling that I can contribute. I don't need to keep score to know when I do."

At every opportunity Cindy reinforced this doctrine. "Just Do It" would have been a more appropriate marketing slogan for the Mothers of Basketball than it's been for Nike. Just show up Sunday night, just play. Cindy forbade teams from holding practices, and she relentlessly congratulated everyone for those final scores of 0–0, especially in her column in the group's monthly newsletter. "We continue to enjoy winning without losing, and occasionally risking our dignity for a loose ball or a 'critical' rebound," she wrote in one typically unapologetic briefing. "I am especially proud of the fact that even our best players find immense satisfaction in playing just to play."

At the Jewish Community Center the men in charge at first would not allow Cindy's group to use the whole gym, and later they told her in no uncertain terms that her utopian approach was doomed by the oncoming tide of competitive women. They warned her that she would have to adjust if she wanted to survive. She told them if they were so sure of that, they should form a women's league of their own. "They tried," Cindy said. "They failed."

Cindy liked to compare her league to a product with a specially targeted audience. If she modified it to accommodate the scorekeeping mentality, the male model, she would likely lose a good percentage of her core clientele. There were other leagues as close as fifteen minutes away that kept score; there were no others like hers. "I have always run this league where I will solicit your opinion but I will make the decision," she said. "Very rarely will I bring up an issue and leave it to others."

Like Lisa Ciardi, Cindy had never previously thought of herself as a natural leader. She still tended to amaze herself when she held the three versus three tournament (in which scores were kept) at the conclusion of every season, and there would be at least sixty women in the gym at once, milling about, and Cindy would order them to be quiet and sit down. Lo and behold, they would shut up and sit.

"Sometimes I think of myself as this poor slob who wanted to start a basketball game, and now I've been on Lifetime television and in *The Washington Post*," she said. "It's mind-boggling to me." Her basketball league had given her shining moments that she had never even considered. She had never been what she called a "hangout person." Now she was, at least many Sunday nights. For her fiftieth birthday the players had made her a cake, taken her out for pizza, hired a fortune-teller.

She didn't mind that several of the younger players and even some of the older ones really preferred to keep score. She had to admit to counting her own points in her head because "it wasn't like it was that many." It was all right to have an ego, but if it was for the purpose of feeling good, for self-esteem, didn't that prove her point? What more could a scoreboard tell you that you didn't already know?

Diane Perrine, a fifty-eight-year-old grandmother, disagreed, saying she preferred that shot of adrenaline created by a fear of losing. She got her score fix from a local church league and from playing tennis three times a week. She remained a MOB member in good standing for the exercise, the friendships. "I wouldn't give it up in a million years," she said. "A lot of the younger ones come in and say we should keep score, but in the end they realize they're getting a lot out of this without it."

Diane had been playing basketball as far back as college at William and Mary, but usually in a place where the guys couldn't see, where they couldn't jump to the conclusion that she must be a lesbian. "There's no other way to say it," she said. "William and Mary was a southern school, and we couldn't let the boys know we loved to play sports."

Now she coached girls and was thrilled to see that the athletes—and not the "pretty little prom queens"—were the most popular girls in school. But Diane acknowledged that Cindy did have a niche, because no matter how level the playing field was getting, many of today's young female athletes would eventually have to find that delicate balance between their competitive nature and Mother Nature. After bearing children they might very well decide they needed something closer to risk- and stress-free. "The ones over thirty start crossing the line from 'I'm going to kill you so you won't score' to 'I really like basketball but I don't want to get hurt,'" Cindy said.

They saw Cindy's light, and new potential benefits. Kate Magnuson, in her early thirties, had played college ball and had initially made it clear that she wouldn't mind keeping score. Her husband and brothers couldn't believe that she would waste her time playing without it. Then her mother, Caroline Owens, decided to try the game for the first time in her mid-fifties. Kate realized that Caroline never would have wanted to "enter a two-point game in the final two minutes." This league was perfect for her, for them; mother and daughter played one year on the same team. They went out for drinks. Their adult relationship, already close, grew closer.

In another family affair Diane Lewis's eight-year-old daughter, Shawn Marie, was the timekeeper for her game one Sunday night. She cheered along with the players on the blue and white teams when her mother took a pass and banked in a layup at the buzzer, a game-ending shot that once upon a time might have set her off on a wild celebration. Now Diane just jogged off deliberately, carrying the support of a full brace on her left knee.

Almost two decades earlier Diane had been a local high school star at T. C. Williams in Alexandria, with a full scholarship on the table from American University. As a high school senior she tore ligaments in her left knee. She never did get to take the scholarship. She never played college ball. She went to Old Dominion instead, watching wistfully from the stands as Nancy Lieberman made her team a national champion and herself into a national sports celebrity.

By the time she was married and working as a loan officer, Diane had had surgery on the knee. It would never be perfect, but it was certainly good enough to play recreationally. The day she signed up with Cindy's league, Diane was one of its best players. She had the ranginess of a player. She walked and jogged and dribbled like one. Then she went out on the court and tore all the ligaments again.

Diane needed more surgery, but that had been four years ago, and she hadn't bothered yet. She couldn't go through with it, couldn't afford the long recovery time, given the demands of work and family. "I can't turn or cut," she said. "I've had to teach myself how to play differently, without lateral movement."

There was no point in her playing in the advanced league, so she resided happily in the MOB minors, where, even with her limited mobility, she was by far one of the most skilled players. It didn't matter; she wasn't playing anymore for championships or scholarships. For Diane, once one of the lucky ones, that was as much a distant dream as it was for any woman who had been relegated to the sidelines for no reason other than that she was female.

Bonnie Clark (not her real name) was a classic case, a girl who loved sports in the 1950s but sat on the side, rooting for three brothers, wishing there was something for her in or around Scranton, Pennsylvania. There wasn't. Her brothers' Little League teams would occasionally let her practice, but the sport she really wanted to try was basketball. This was the game she loved, for its fast pace, for the almost balletlike quality of a player in midflight. "In all my years of watching my brothers and watching the game on television and now going to the WNBA games, I've always thought, If there was one thing I wish I could do, it would be to go up in the air and hit the jumper," she said. "The jump shot to me was always a thing of beauty." By the time she found a place to play, in Cindy's league, the jump shot remained Bonnie's unattainable dream because of a real-life nightmare.

It was back in the 1970s, after purchasing a house in a gritty area of Washington, D.C., she hoped would gentrify, that she came home one night to find four men in the house, and a gun to her stomach. They dragged her to an abandoned school, where they sexually assaulted her, leaving her bruised, disoriented, barefoot, groping in the dark to find her way out. "There were boarded-up windows, but I came upon one that was just open," she said. "It was so dark, I couldn't see the ground when I looked out."

She heard a noise behind her and panicked. One of the rapists had come back. She had no time to think, only to react. She went out the window. As it turned out it was just a short drop, but she landed barefoot on cement. Her ankle was crushed. It had been almost twenty years since doctors placed screws in Bonnie's ankle to hold it together. She still couldn't run, or even walk, without a limp. She certainly couldn't shoot the jumper.

Bonnie played tough defense, though, sometimes too tough for this kind of league, and when her ankle limited her playing time, she went back to the sideline, back to rooting. She wasn't playing this season, and didn't know if she would again. The truth was, from all those years watching her brothers play, all she had ever really known in sports was partisanship, and that had made the no-score concept difficult for her to enjoy.

She had to admit, though, it worked better for many of the others, and the bottom line was that at least they had a place to play, under conditions and terms they all could meet. Most of all, best of all, here was an example of women setting rules for women, and having the power to enforce them.

THE PLAYER CINDY had promised to keep an eye on apparently got the message and toned down her physical play. The problem seemed to be resolved, and the night appeared to be developing crisis-free when players from one of the teams surrounded Cindy and began complaining about excessive bye weeks in the schedule. What could she do, Cindy asked. People wanted to play, and there was only so much gym time available. "Women are amazing," she said, after the plaintiffs left in a huff. "They don't hesitate to complain. They drive me crazy."

After settling countless disputes over ten years, Cindy had begun letting go of her baby, hoping it would go on without her. At the midcentury mark of life, she was tiring of playing nursemaid to the women, many of whom were now almost two decades younger than she. Sandy Mayer, a real nurse, had already assumed much of the administrative responsibility for the advanced league.

Sandy was as close to a handpicked successor and soul mate as Cindy was going to find. Though she had played basketball in high school, Sandy had no more desire to keep score than Cindy did. At forty-two, the mother of young children, she also had more resolve than Cindy had left to keep fighting, particularly the men at the Jewish Community Center who continued to lean on them to change.

Sandy stewed when they sneered at the suggested rules Cindy had drafted to eliminate physical play after several contentious incidents. Cindy and Sandy maintained that the women should accept the more passive style of play or go elsewhere. They decided that the first time a player was cited by an official, she would get a warning; the second time, she would be asked to leave the game. A third time, it would be suggested that she depart the league.

"The JCC director said, 'Why don't you just have five fouls?'" Sandy recounted. "But it's the way they say it, as if we're being ridiculous just trying to come up with a way that works better for us."

What in the world made men so certain that their way was the right way, she asked. The Mothers of Basketball happened to be more than a sports league; it was also a self-contained community, a support group. The older women, Sandy said, seemed to want more than a few moments a week of personal glory from their sports experience. More than any basket she would ever score, Sandy said she would remember the personal touches, the going-away parties for teammates, the way they rallied to the support of a league mate who'd miscarried.

She was determined to preserve Cindy's legacy, at least until she and her family relocated to New Jersey, just outside Philadelphia, during the summer of 2000. Then Sandy went hunting for a gymnasium, for new teammates and soul mates, in an attempt to start a brand-new league.

Back in Virginia, Cindy began the process of choosing another administrator who stopped counting at zero. "As long as the league is run by people I put in place, nobody will change it," she said. "But this is only a moment in time. Our generation is getting on. We will go away. This mentality will probably be overtaken. I keep telling my friends we'll have to keep it alive in a wheelchair league."

For now Cindy was back to the drawing board, planning a new home for herself, an over-forty league for the coming winter. The over-thirties was getting too crowded with women who, even upon acceptance of her rules, were too much younger and faster, with a greater capacity for developing skills. "These are not obnoxious women, in any way," Cindy said. "But it's so obvious. They instinctively know how to pass and know where to be on the other end of the pass. For the most part they're happy to have me play with them, but if our whole league becomes like the advanced league, if there's more of them than there are of us, I'm not going to be comfortable. I'm not a good basketball player, but I still want to have the chance to play."

She didn't mind having to move on, because she had become used to finding or just inventing a place for herself. Off the soccer field, into the intermediate league, into the planned over-forties, and all the way into that wheelchair, if necessary—for the pre–Title IXer it was like being a squatter, always having to scatter when the young urban professionals came to redevelop the property. They'd had years of shining moments. Cindy had color war.

"This I know I can do," she said her first time at Camp AWOL, stepping onto the volleyball court. Then it was her turn to serve, and she couldn't get the ball over the net. "I felt like a mere shadow of myself, or at least of the image that I had of myself as a child," she said.

She asked Nora Silver, "Did I only imagine that I was a decent athlete as a kid?" Her old friend told her, "How long has it been since you served a volleyball? You're comparing yourself to women who have been playing since they were little."

She knew better than to compare. Yet sometimes, even with wisdom and the most benign expectations, you couldn't help it. You couldn't just get out of the way even when common sense was dictating you should. You had to take a stand, and compete.

11

Alphas and Betas

T HEY WERE LIKE KIDS on the first day of school, nervous and excited and a little uncertain of where to go and
how to act and how demanding the new teacher would be.
"No more Betas," Filip Bondy, the new Pokémoms' coach, told his
players as they stretched along the sideline. "Time to be Alphas."

This was easy for him to say. For years he had coached his now
college-age son on elite travel teams, and his teenage daughter had
played a variety of sports well from early elementary school on.
These mothers of intention, so determined to play for fairness and
fun, had never been in the position of having a team depend on them
for much more than support, a pass, a defensive blockade. And while
not as skilled as the open league, the intermediate division was no
beginner level either; it was still cut from the Darwinian mold.

Here, while there was less risk of being taken out with a hard slide, the teams had still done their own recruiting and had no self-imposed mandate to deemphasize results.

Tonight's opponent to open the fall season, the Sisters of Soccer, or SOS, had taken on several younger players, including one with frizzy, dark hair tied back and a pair of baggy blue shorts that drooped near her knees. "It's Ms. Schwartz," Beth Fuqua said, doing a double take.

Barrie Schwartz, twenty-five, was a third-grade teacher at the Bradford School who had played the game growing up on Long Island until she was injured in high school. It had been ten years since she'd last played competitive soccer, but some childhood habits, like riding a bike or dribbling around a slow-reacting defender, you never do forget.

It therefore took less than a minute for Barrie to control a pass, size up the defense, push right with the dribble, and rifle a right-footed shot against the grain and past a stunned Cathy Wright.

The Pokémoms, alive with chatter for the start of their season, were suddenly subdued, with the exception of Nina Sloan. "It's OK, Cathy," she called out from the bench, where she was serving her one-game suspension for the red card she'd received in the now infamous Ravan incident. "It's just one goal." Soon, however, it was two goals, then three, four, and, by halftime, five. Five–nothing after one half! In the goddamned intermediate league!

It wasn't Cathy's fault. She was obviously a runner, a field player, not a goalie, at least not one in Nina's class. When the half ended, the entire team surrounded her and hugged her, grateful that she had volunteered for target practice until Nina could play the following week.

After her long summer of soul-searching, Nina had decided to move down with the Pokémoms. It was flattering to have been wanted by the younger, more skilled players, but these women were her age, her peers, her friends. And if the Pokémoms as a group were perhaps a bit too idealistic, the scuffle with Ravan had brought out something in Nina that she wished to lock away forever. Soccer— sports—just shouldn't be that important, she reasoned, in a full and balanced adult life. Besides, when she mentioned to Beth Fuqua that she really didn't want to be stuck in goal for every minute of every game, Beth told her not to worry, they would all take turns so she could get out and run.

That, of course, was before the Pokémoms began to realize the consequences of choosing a team wholly on the basis of attitude, not ability. That was before they discovered that, even in the intermediate league, there were young terriers like Barrie Schwartz, who resumed her scoring binge in the second half, barely taking a minute to rest on the bench, though victory was already guaranteed.

It is one thing not to let losing ruin your week. It's another thing to casually accept being embarrassed. So Beth Albert, back on defense, may have, purely out of frustration, gotten a little too physical trying to keep Barrie from scoring yet again.

Barrie wheeled suddenly and snarled, "Get your fucking hands off me, Beth."

Beth backed away, her ears shading red. "You don't have to swear," she stammered.

Barrie was a teacher, by gosh, and there were children on the sideline, including Beth's boys, Alex and Charlie, who were students in Barrie's school, at which Beth was also a dignitary. "Some respect, please, for the PTA president," someone yelled out from the Poké-mom bench, resulting in a chorus of hoots and giggles.

Barrie later apologized, and much later was recruited by Beth A. to teach soccer in an after-school program. But her more immediate response was to deposit another goal into the net. Not that the Poké-moms, careening helplessly toward a double-digit defeat, were still counting.

"I feel like I'm going to cry," Beth Fuqua said, coming off after a second-half shift, exhausted by the sheer misery of her team barely being able to clear the ball from its own end. She was out of breath and actually fighting tears, already feeling the weight of responsibility for the ongoing rout, for the team she had picked, three Beths and a dozen Betas. "If every game is going to be like this . . ." she said.

Ellen Paretti tried to cheer her up with the power of positive thinking. "Beth [Albert] says she does this with her kids," Ellen said. "Just try to remember the one thing you did tonight that you liked the best."

Granted, Ellen conceded, there wasn't going to be much to choose from, though the Pokémoms' bench did break into approving applause after Nancy Parlapiano's breakaway and goal late in the game—albeit for the SOS.

Nancy was mobbed by her teammates, and as Filip noted out of the side of his mouth, "That's a lot of celebrating for an eighth or ninth goal."

"Oh, it's OK," Beth Panucci said. "It's Nancy." Who happened to be another Bradford School parent, mother of three, and good friend to several Pokémoms.

Filip, feigning the role of the frustrated jock, said, "I may as well slit my wrists right now." Instead, he conducted an impromptu chalk talk along the sideline after the game ended, mercifully. In the absence of natural shooters, the Pokémoms would have to focus on positioning, he said. The women stared back at him, respecting his expertise but unconvinced they could put it to use. They would again go scoreless the following week against the Chicks with Cleats, though Nina's presence in goal would help keep the score to a respectable 3–0. "We have to remember we're doing this for the first time," she said afterward. "We're not the Bluestone Belles."

Which reminded Barbara that Lisa had called her and asked if the Pokémoms might want to scrimmage some Sunday morning in the park. "She's asked me twice," Barbara said. "The first time I didn't say anything, but then she asked again, so I'd better give her an answer."

Here they had just lost their first two games in the intermediate league without scoring a goal. Did the Pokémoms really need another assault on their reeling egos in a scrimmage against Lisa's team of Alphas?

Oh, what the hell, it would just be a scrimmage, just practice, they decided. They were all friends, weren't they? "Maybe," Ellen said, hopefully, "we'll just choose up sides."

S ITTING ALONG THE SIDELINE, waiting for the eight o'clock game to finish, Ravan looked up to see Meg pushing her way through the revolving door from the lobby that led onto the field. "Here to root for the Badgers?" Ravan asked.

"For everyone," said Meg.

"No freakin' way," Ravan said, her ubiquitous baseball cap turned backwards.

Meg just laughed. If she were really intending to root for the Badgers in their first fall meeting against Lisa's team, she would have to be discreet about it, now that she'd planted both feet in the management camp alongside Ashley. Meg was still a regular at the clinics in the park, which were being run by two coaches freshly imported from England, Vanessa Hardwick and Kevin McGrath. Lisa and Meg were probably the two women who attended most regularly, and they had moved way beyond even the bread-breaking breakfast and were becoming friends. Their fourth-graders, John and Andrew, had wound up on the same U-10 travel team. They almost had no choice but to become car-pooling cronies.

Meg said she might play again down the road, but for now, at least, she needed to step back. Anna Girdwood wasn't playing for the Badgers either, an even more damaging loss; Ashley and his staff had thought it better if his coaches did not participate. Anna coached some of the daughters of these women, on travel teams, in weeklong camps. In light of the battles previously fought, the lessons already learned, it didn't make professional sense to be competing against their mothers. So Anna was now the Badgers' coach.

In addition, Connie Meola was on maternity leave, and Amy Roy, the team's founder, was concentrating on her photography and her latest sports venture—partnership with Tony Meola in a soccer merchandise store in the Watchung Plaza shopping section of Montclair.

The Badgers were in transition, and Ravan was in turmoil. "We don't have Anna, and they have new players, younger players," she said, suspiciously eyeing Lisa's gang a few feet away. "When I heard that there was recruiting going on, that made me crazy, because I want to win."

It was true that the recruiting had become intense, and that by late summer the Monday night game in the park had become something of a meat market, with the captains of various teams keeping an eye out for new blood dropping in unannounced.

Her roster still short by early September, Lisa had had the good fortune to land three experienced players, including Karen Bredlaw, a twenty-four-year-old former player at Bethany College in West Virginia. Karen had played some coed games with Jeanne Jeffrey, who led her to the Monday night game and right to Lisa.

Not only had Karen played since she was five years old, she had been a starter on the boys' team at South Allegheny High School in football-crazed Pittsburgh, where, even in the early 1990s, there was still no girls' soccer team.

"I had probably the best passing skills on the team, because that's what I had to do," she said. "I wasn't as big or aggressive as the guys. I had to think more. I was the one who made the perfect cross."

Lisa's two other new players were childhood friends, Kris Smith and Grace Rhinesmith, from a town north of Montclair.

Six feet tall with a blistering shot, Kris made her presence felt immediately with a timely cross to Clare Moore for a goal past Minnie Evans and an early 2–1 lead against the Badgers. "Nice pass, Grace," Dana yelled out from the bench.

"That's Kris," said Ginger, handling the substitutions for the former Bluestone Belles, who were now calling themselves . . .

"What are we calling ourselves, anyway?" Dana asked.

Team X wouldn't fly. Bob Stanton, one of Ashley's staffers who was appointed manager of the women's leagues, called Lisa and told her to pick a name already. Lisa, somewhat befuddled, went from X to Xtreme.

This at least fit the pattern of a league getting younger, more competitive and contemporary; with rare exceptions younger women who had grown up thinking of themselves as athletes did not fancy themselves Sisters of Soccer or Beanie Babes. For them sports weren't about being clever or cute; they wanted team names that symbolized action and attitude. So the Pride became the Madness. The younger Pokémoms became the Rave, evolving from card and cartoon characters to clubby trendsetters.

Belles to Xtreme, if nothing else, characterized Lisa as soccer-playing-mom-to-the-max. The Xtreme didn't have snazzy jerseys, didn't have jerseys at all, outfitting themselves in an assortment of ragged gray T-shirts and tank tops. But even dressed down, with Sarah Hogan out with an injury and Mary Burke in goal, it was clear that Lisa had upgraded her roster, and the Badgers had not kept pace.

Her team trailing 3–2 in the second half, Ravan tried to dribble out of her own end, but Venera used her much longer legs to poke the ball away. While Ravan theatrically rolled over and tried to create the impression she'd been tripped, Venera rifled a shot into the right corner of the net. Then Kris Smith scored on a penalty shot, and the game was out of reach.

The mood had changed between these teams, though. This game had none of the tension, the sheer animosity of the previous Badgers–Belles tussles. Part of it was the Xtreme's superiority. Part of it was that the novelty had worn off. Whatever, the atmosphere could almost be described as fraternal. Lisa said she liked it much better.

The Xtreme moved on to the younger competition, beating the Madness, Jen McEwan's and Caroline Quidort's new team, with surprising ease, 5–0. On the third week of the new season, against the Rave, Jeanne Jeffrey absentmindedly caught the ball as if she were the goalie in front of her net—a red-card offense. Down a player for most of the night, the Xtreme nonetheless won that game, too, 3–2.

They were undefeated after the first go-round, quickly establishing themselves as the class of the open league. Sure, the three new, younger players helped, but all the teams had been restyled, upgraded, and even someone as competitive as Jen McEwan had to concede that the Xtreme had something the younger women did not.

"They're very dedicated about this," she said. "I have to give them credit the way they go to the soccer moms' clinics, practice every week. You can see the difference watching them play, as opposed to us. We don't have the communication, the cohesion. Soccer is less about being individually better than it is about being better as a team."

Mary Burke, who was preparing to leave Montclair for a three-month vacation in Australia, was not surprised that the erstwhile Team X was playing with an unmistakable identity. There was something Lisa brought to her team—a commitment, a passion—that Mary didn't sense with the others. "The new players just blended in with the older ones, with the same spirit we had from last spring," she said. "I think that the closeness off the field carries over onto it. Lisa cares so much more about her team. Most of the women who play with her are together so much of the time."

The going-away party for Mary at Venera Gashi's made her feel she was being sent off on her journey by family, by loved ones. Drinks at Tierney's. Coffee after morning clinics. Play dates with the kids. Strategy sessions back of the Bradford School while Lisa and Ginger were waiting for dismissal. "Our communication is so much better, our passing, but it's more than just a physical thing," Mary said.

The reality was that the Xtreme wasn't that much better than its competition, but with togetherness came a trust, a belief, a sense that they were the best team because they were greater than the sum of their parts. Successful sports teams at every level of competition feel this quality more easily than they can explain it.

The power, though, was inexplicably fleeting, a surge of collective excellence that was as difficult to hold on to as air itself. "When I'm in goal and looking out over the field, I can see it, I really can, but I almost can't describe it," Mary said. Then she did, and with the eloquence of an Irish poet. "It's like we're a bouquet of flowers," she said. "Flowers in a vase."

S TEVE COOK had told her that she wouldn't believe it, and only now, as she watched the soccer dome fill with women and children, all dressed in shorts and cleats and ready to play, did it dawn on Vanessa Hardwick that this was a place she needed to come.

It was the first Saturday night in November, and Ashley and Meg had opened the doors of the dome for a family celebration, the anniversary of the first soccer moms' clinic. The actual date had been October 21, and it would likely have passed unnoticed had Beth

Fuqua not walked up to Lisa back of the Bradford School that afternoon and given her a hug and kiss. "Congratulations," Beth said. "It's our one-year soccer anniversary."

A light went on in Lisa's head when someone suggested a party, which the soccer moms were always up for. She asked Beth Albert, the public relations expert, if she would make a request to Ashley to open the dome. Beth called, and Ashley liked the idea. He immediately circulated a flyer announcing the "First Annual Soccer Moms' Appreciation Night."

At the bottom, under the heading "Soccer Mom Facts," it said: "Nothing is so powerful as an idea whose time had come." In keeping with that feminist theme, Ashley's plan was to inform the attending husbands that their assignments for the evening were to supervise the refreshments in the lobby and help run the arts and crafts group for the children too young to play.

But first, before the balls were rolled out, he and Meg had one significant presentation to make. "This all started in this town with one person," Ashley said, the mothers and children sitting on the field, all bunched together. He asked Lisa to come up and presented her with a black sweatshirt with the Ashley's Soccer Camp inscription on the upper-left corner. "Thanks to you," he said, "we have the best soccer moms in the country."

Lisa, practically blushing, posed for snapshots with Ashley and Meg, pictures that further demonstrated how Lisa and Meg had become teammates within a much larger and more significant clan.

As she officiated the mothers' full-field scrimmage that capped off the evening, with the kids and husbands cheering madly from the sideline, Vanessa thought how "brilliant" it was for these women to have created such an outlet. It was amazing what was happening with women's soccer in this town, this country.

Her old friend Steve Cook had been right when he told her that if anyone could appreciate it, if anyone needed to see it, it was

Vanessa. So she had taken his advice: She had signed a contract with Ashley's Soccer Camp to come to New Jersey, and it was a big story in the London newspapers, one of which draped her in the Stars and Stripes under the headline VANESSA DROPS FA FOR USA.

Vanessa Hardwick, a thirty-four-year-old teacher and lifelong lover of sport, was quite the media celebrity in London, the self-described "poster girl for the women's cause." All she had really wanted was a coaching license from the FA, or Football Association, after putting in the required time in the field and the classroom. But in England, where soccer is religion and where males are considered soldiers of the faith while the FA plays God, Vanessa had discovered the harsh realities of challenging a deity and its insatiable hunger for status quo. The FA was a huge organization with no equal opportunity policy, Vanessa said. It had a long history of keeping women out, including banning them from the FA-sanctioned grounds after thousands of women started playing soccer during World War I.

When Vanessa began her pursuit, there were few women's teams and fewer women licensed by the FA. She kept flunking the course, when it was obvious to her and others whose judgments were unbiased, many of them licensed male coaches, that she was good enough to pass. "There were simple ways they managed it," she said. "They would tell me not to do certain things during the coaching exams. Then they would say, 'Why didn't you do those things?'"

She thought of dropping the whole issue, of permanently shifting her athletic focus to basketball, the sport she began playing in her twenties for lack of access to soccer. She suspected that the English would never allow women to breach their sacred territory but felt a surprising and unexplainable defiant streak in her.

All Vanessa knew was that she was really good at coaching and wasn't going to be dismissed without a fight. On her own she decided to seek legal recourse, prepared to defend herself if need be.

Luckily, her teachers' union agreed to support her financially, to underwrite a lawyer and a public relations adviser for a story certain to attract major attention. For two years, from September 1997 to May 4, 1999, Vanessa Hardwick became the woman who took on the big, bad FA.

And she won, sort of, when the Employment Tribunal decided in her favor, ordering the Football Association to pay almost £15,000 in special damages and compensation. Unfortunately, the tribunal only recommended that Vanessa receive her advanced coaching license within twenty-eight days of the decision, or the FA would be required to pay an additional £9,675 in damages. Defiant to the end, the FA paid the money, refusing to give in to the woman who at the time had what the media reported was the second-highest qualification in the country, based on experience and test results.

Drained by her long struggle, mourning the recent loss of her mother to cancer, Vanessa found herself in desperate need of a change of scenery. She left her teacher's job behind and signed on for one year with Ashley's company. She arrived in the States in late August, scared and lonely, holed up in an apartment she would share with two of the other coaches, Kevin McGrath and Karen Sherris, wondering what in the world she had got herself into.

She soon met some of the soccer moms, including Lisa Ciardi, whom she liked right away. Lisa may have had three young children, but in fact she was only four years older; there was something about Lisa, an introverted and vulnerable quality that Vanessa related to. She understood perfectly why Lisa, who at her parents' insistence had become a competent pianist but could not bring herself to play a note in front of almost anyone, nonetheless relished the opportunity to perform on the field.

They were about the same height, similar build, dark hair streaked with gray. Lisa wasn't loud or pushy, yet there was a determination, a purpose about her. What Vanessa most recognized was that they were both athletic women who had been cheated long enough and who had come to the conclusion that they weren't going to be Betas anymore.

They naturally became friends. Vanessa was invited for coffee by day and to Tierney's by night. Lisa talked her into playing with the Xtreme in a more informal Sunday night indoor league in nearby West Orange. Vanessa quickly fell in with Lisa's core group. It lightened her adjustment to America. She was most grateful for that.

Later in the fall they went to the Continental Airlines Arena to watch the U.S. Women's World Cup team on its victory tour against European all-star teams. Vanessa couldn't believe the crowd, the mothers and daughters, the sheer idolatry of the girls in the Mia Hamm jerseys. Just months before, back home, she would have needed a magnifying glass to find a single score from the Women's World Cup in those same papers that could never get enough of her struggle against the FA. But that was muckraking. This was soccer, women's soccer. American women had much to be thankful for. "You'd never get a crowd like that in England for women," Vanessa said. "The attitudes are so different over here."

She didn't know how long she was going to stay. She missed her father, her sister, her friends. But Steve Cook had been right, she realized on the night when the Montclair soccer mothers acknowledged their anniversary in the dome, the way Mia Hamm and company had their World Cup victory. This was the perfect place for her to come and heal.

A FTER THREE WEEKS of being shut out, of seldom coming close to the net, the Pokémoms finally scored a goal. And the only thing Brandi Chastain had on any of them when it came to celebration was that they managed to keep their shirts on.

They were already losing to the Beanie Babes, 3–0, when the big event occurred. Beth Panucci, who normally played defense, was up in the offensive end, and Diane Gray had the ball on the left side. Diane crossed it to Beth, who was open in the middle, about twenty feet in front of the net. Hearing the mantra Filip had by now drilled into all of their heads—"just shoot!"—Beth one-timed the ball in the direction of the net.

It skipped merrily along the turf—not exactly a screamer, but the goalie was screened—and the next thing Beth knew the ball was in the left corner of the net.

Beth, who had never scored for the original Pokémoms, cupped her hands over her mouth, then began jumping up and down. Her teammates, including Nina, who rushed upfield from her perch in goal, mobbed her. "Like it was the World Series and everyone swarms the pitcher," Beth said. "It must have looked really strange to the other team."

Actually, the Beanie Babes appeared delighted to have had the Pokémoms finally score. Several applauded, and another yelled out, "You deserve it."

The Pokémoms lost the game 4–1. They were still winless but were certainly relieved they would not be going the entire schedule scoreless. Or winless, as matters would develop the following week.

In the interest of keeping the spirit of the old Belles alive, Lisa showed up to watch her three former teammates play the former Hot Flashes, now known simply as the Flash. So did Mary Burke, who was leaving for Australia within the week. Ellen, Barbara, and Beth Albert were thrilled. Rilee McDonald, a nanny and the one Pokémom who wasn't a mom, had some of her friends drop in as well. With the usual array of husbands and kids, it seemed as if the Pokémoms were playing in a rabid home-field environment.

Was it the fan support? The absence of the Flash's regular goalie after she injured herself in an auto mishap? The law of averages playing out in the Pokémoms' favor? No one could explain the sudden outburst of scoring that produced a 4–0 lead before the end of the first half.

First Rilee scored on a breakaway, sending her little fan club into apoplexy. Soon after, Cathy Wright got her foot into the ball once it became dislodged from a pileup of bodies in front of the net; she scored for a 2–0 lead. And then came what Ellen would later call "the athletic moment of my life," when her feet and the ball and the stars and the moon all must have been perfectly aligned.

Ellen had just gained control of the ball on the right sideline, near midfield, where several of the attending children had one eye on the game and the other on their Game Boys. Now here came one of the Flashes, feet aflutter, bodying up on Ellen. Calmly, elegantly, Ellen turned to shield the ball with her body. Just as the other woman instinctively relaxed, Ellen put the ball on her left foot, spun back around, and flicked it into the open space behind her opponent.

With that slick maneuver she was free, with an unobstructed view of Beth Fuqua up ahead, alone, on the left side. Ellen now switched back to her right foot, her natural side, and made the pass, the perfect lead pass, which Beth controlled on the run. She dribbled within range of the net, behind the last defender, who had been playing up and was surprised by Ellen's playmaking. The shot—the goal itself—was almost anticlimactic. Most memorable was Ellen's true Alpha moment.

"I'm so happy for her," Lisa said. "Look at her. She's so relaxed. If she were still playing in the other league, she would be apologizing all over the place."

Within minutes Beth Fuqua scored again, for a 4–0 lead, at which point there was sentiment on the Pokémoms' bench not to do to the Flash what the SOS had done to them. It was too soon to commiserate, as it turned out. The game was only half over. And it was now Nina's time to come out of the goal.

In her spare time, almost in the way one would enjoy doing the crossword puzzle, Beth Panucci had taken to devising lineups that would play to the team's strength. She loved the challenge, the piecing together of the talents. Knowing most of the players were reluctant to replace Nina in goal, she volunteered herself. Beth was extremely light on her feet, as quick as Nina, but she didn't have the experience and confidence in goal, or Nina's positional instincts. She didn't think like a goalie, as Nina clearly did. She didn't know how to play the angles, and didn't quite have the knack for making those split-second decisions on how far to stray from the net to retrieve a loose ball—crucial on a fast artificial surface and a smaller indoor field.

The first-half results suggested it didn't matter who played goal, but as mysteriously as the offensive power had visited the Poké-moms, it vanished completely. About eight minutes into the second half, the Flash began controlling the play. A shot unleashed from a good thirty feet out caught Beth P. by surprise and made it 4–1. Not long after, a penalty shot was awarded to the Flash, and the conversion made it 4–2.

There were still a good eight minutes left in the game. Filip, who to this point had been content to let the Pokémoms police themselves as much as they cared to, turned to Beth Fuqua on the bench and said that if the Flash scored again, he was going to disregard Beth P.'s lineup and sub Nina back in goal.

Beth F. turned pale.

"But that's not the philosophy of our team," she stammered, worried about how Beth P. would feel being yanked from goal.

"Trust me," Filip said, "she'll feel worse if you lose."

Sure enough, Beth P. soon wandered too far into the corner and wasn't back in time when the ball was crossed. Boom, into the net, 4–3, with still about five minutes to play.

Back into goal went Nina, with Ellen and Cathy on defense. While Beth P., clearly upset, was consoled on the bench, it became apparent in the final, tense minutes that the Pokémoms would have lost the lead and likely the game had Nina not returned to the net. She made at least three saves that Beth P. would not have made, including one diving stop off a header, and another when she was positioned perfectly to block the deflection of a corner kick angled beautifully to the right post.

When the game was over, Nina made sure first to find Beth P. for a much-needed hug. There were smiles all around and even a few telling concessions as they rounded up the kids and headed out to their cars.

"When they got to 4–3, I realized how much I really wanted to win," Rochelle Sandler said.

"Me, too," Beth F. said. "I guess I have to admit that I'm more competitive than I thought."

These concessions reflected nothing more than human nature; the women had realized it was quite all right, during the game, to risk the feelings of an individual for the benefit of the team as long as it was done with care. Beth P. later said it was obvious to her that the Pokémoms needed Nina back in goal, but she didn't want to take herself out and put the pressure of saving the game on someone else.

Fortunately, they'd had Filip to make the decision for them. But he had agreed to coach them only for the fall season. His travel schedule for the *Daily News* was hectic; his goal was to get the Pokémoms to the point where they could govern themselves—and stop being so single-minded in their approach.

He wasn't suggesting they go home and punish themselves for losing with sit-ups and no bedtime snack. It was enough to admit that sports were about winning and losing, making good plays and bad . . . once in a while, anyway.

A couple of weeks later the Pokémoms were playing the Beanie Babes, and Ellen, dribbling in the midfield, tried to loop the ball toward the goal. She shanked it wide, out of bounds.

"Nice kick, Ellen," Beth Albert yelled out, only to have Filip snap, "That wasn't a good kick. You can't patronize players. How will they ever know the difference?" This set off a lively sideline debate, with Beth A. and Barbara asserting that they had always preferred coaches for their children who didn't criticize mistakes, and Filip responding that those kids would consequently never learn from them.

Finally, Rochelle piped up that Ellen was obviously smart enough to know the difference between a good play and a bad one, but Filip should understand that women—at least women of their generation—habitually needed to put a positive spin on things. "That," she said, effectively settling the argument, "is how we stay married to men."

W ITH EACH PASSING MINUTE, with every shot that went whistling past Giselle Petraroia's shoulders and head, with every hoot 'n' holler that came from the Xtreme bench, Jen McEwan saw a deeper shade of red. She didn't know what the score was anymore, and didn't much care—that was how badly the Madness was losing. "Something to one," Jeanne Jeffrey said from the small bleachers across the field from the Madness bench when Ellen Paretti asked.

Jeanne was serving her one-game suspension for catching the ball in the goal area against the Rave. She was explaining what had happened to Ravan Magrath, who had stayed after playing in the early game. Sitting to Jeanne's right was Ellen, who had dropped in to hand off an Anne Lamott novel to her partner-in-literature, Wendy Cogdell of the Rave, and to see how her old friends were doing.

On this night they were doing great, and not so great. They had come with their full complement of players to find the Madness with only six team members and one recruit from the intermediate league so they could field a squad. Caroline Quidort was away for several weeks. Another of their players had broken an ankle. One was ill. One or two were not reliable. Jen had called the dome earlier in the week to let it be known that they would not have enough players. She said she was told by one of the staff to bring a player from the intermediate league—he was sure it would be all right.

But it wasn't, at least it wasn't with Lisa, who felt there was no rule that allowed teams to add players not on their official roster. Even under these circumstances, she argued that allowing the Madness to use Joyce Milano, who normally played with Chicks with Cleats, would establish an unhealthy precedent, an unwanted pickup game mentality. "It wasn't my place to say the rules should change," Lisa said. "Then the Madness said, Let's play six versus six, but I said, That's not fair to our players, who made the commitment."

This was, to Lisa, the whole point. She, more than anyone, had made the commitment, the phone calls. She had made sure that her players were available most Wednesdays, so someone like Jeanne Jeffrey would not have to play fifty hard minutes and she would not be scrambling around, worried whether there would be enough women to play. She had gone to the captains' meetings, made sure players received every bit of information they needed.

Even Jen conceded this was a fundamental difference in the way the older women administered their teams. They were more organized, and she had to admit this was likely the by-product of their not having grown up with everything done for them. Most of them had a lot of practice, she noted, coordinating family affairs.

The old Pride had been a smoother operation with Lori McNamara in charge. "She was excellent, handled everything, didn't take shit from anyone, but when Lori quit it fell on me," Jen said. "I can delegate, but I can't organize." Things were deteriorating so much for the Madness that Caroline and Jen had even asked Lori to come back just as their coach or manager. Lori said she'd think about it, but for now, and on this night against the well-tooled Xtreme, they were on their own, shorthanded and ill-tempered.

Sure, it would have been more sporting for Lisa to have allowed Joyce to fill in as a one-time concession, or to play a six versus six. It would have been truer to her nature, but, damn, these younger women had all the advantages in the first place; why should the rules be modified because they couldn't organize themselves? How many times had she steered to other teams players she might have grabbed herself? Even Jen admitted that when Lori quit it was Lisa who helped replenish the Madness roster to replace the mothers who had moved down.

Lisa decided to stick to her guns, though she knew that the game itself would be as much fun as punishing her kids. "I dreaded going to the dome all day," she said.

From Jen's perspective, she could have forfeited the game and it would have gone into the books as a 3–0 defeat, inflicting much less damage in their goals-against ledger than the 9–1 final that promised to loom large as a potential tiebreaker for the league title.

"When it got out of hand, they should have stopped scoring goals," she said after summoning her friend Karen Sherris and storming off. "You're taught that as kids, and they as mothers should have known better. It got embarrassing and frustrating."

It also got physical, with elbows flying and bodies falling, and then it occurred to Ellen that she was lucky, damned lucky, to be a Pokémom after all. "I'm so happy I'm not playing in this league," she said. "They don't look like they're having fun."

Not that night, and certainly not when the Madness got a rematch several weeks later at full strength. The Xtreme won again, 2–0, but Caroline, back from her hiatus, had gotten the full report on the 9–1 blowout from Jen. A big, physical player to begin with, Caroline leveled Clare Moore in the ribs in front of the net on one play with such force that Clare, on her doctor's advice, wouldn't play for months.

The following week the Xtreme completed a fall season in which they lost no games and tied one by defeating the Badgers, by now the best friends they had left. After the trophy presentation they all headed for Tierney's, where Minnie Evans and some of her Badger teammates lined shots up along the bar and toasted the winners. Who, in turn, toasted them.

To friendship.

To soccer moms.

To keeping the young ones in line, for as long as they possibly could.

12

Leading Ladies

"SOCCER," Sally Maynard was saying, only a few hours after returning home from another visit to the doctor, "is certainly stressful, at least physically." Yet she was determined to continue playing, despite being treated for an ongoing stomach problem, a nervous condition, and an unsettling bout with depression. "The doctor hasn't said I shouldn't play," Sally reported. "But I try to stay back on defense because the way I've been feeling, and at my age, it's hard to play forward."

More difficult for Sally, at sixty-two, was the notion of giving up something she had only recently discovered and wished she could have had years ago. What fun field hockey had been when she played back in high school—more than forty years ago—but what, she rhetorically asked, had been available for her beyond that?

An outdoors lover, Sally as an adult had played tennis and skied and hiked and, in recent years, with her friend Marlene Wasirick, had developed a predilection for bird watching. That was the beauty of being recently retired after thirty-eight years in sales, was it not? Sally had all the time in the world—maybe too much, given the way she was feeling lately. Yet whatever the root of her ailments, whatever muscle aches soccer had wrought, she wasn't about to give up her night at the dome, for no other activity had provided the collective benefits, the delightful socializing, to this unmarried woman who lived alone in nearby Orange.

"Come on out for a bite," the younger women would invariably say after their clinic and game on Tuesday night, beginners' night, for which she had signed up, quite by chance and not without trepidation, in the fall of '99.

Often, after looking in on her ninety-one-year-old mother in the Glen Ridge home Sally had grown up in, she would take a walk through Brookdale Park, and that was where she'd stumbled upon the soccer tournament one day. She was impressed by the sheer volume of kids, and especially by the number of girls. She was amazed by how fast, how fit they all seemed, and how they positioned themselves and passed the ball as if communicating by telepathy. Sally found the whole scene fascinating, and she stayed around long enough and chatted up enough people to learn that the local soccer scene even included programs for women. "You should try it," one of the young female coaches said.

"I'm past my sixtieth birthday," Sally said, waiting to be talked into it.

Well, it turned out that Sally was the oldest, and Marlene, who was in her fifties and joined along with her, was runner-up in the seniors' rankings. It took courage to try to keep up with women who, in some cases, were thirty years younger, even if they were beginners like Sally. But she loved it. The one-hour clinic was a challenge, a gas, and then they would all stay around and watch the women from

Livingston march in to play a live game. To Sally and the other beginners, the Livingston women had at first looked experienced, self-assured, even a bit threatening, but as Barbara Schwindel said, "We could tell them a few stories."

Barbara had been a member of the original Livingston team that debuted at the dome the previous spring without the benefit of a single clinic and wandered into the middle of the Badgers–Belles war. One go-around in the schedule had been enough to send them back to Livingston, presumably forever.

"The other teams, especially the Badgers and the Belles, were so strong, so athletic, so rough," Barbara said. "Most of us were out of breath, and the dome looked so big, and nobody had to tell us that we didn't belong."

But even in recognizing that they were out of their league, open or intermediate, something about the game had inspired them. In the ensuing months they occasionally reconvened to kick the ball around and wonder what they might do to create their own space. "One day I said, 'Everyone should call someone you know,'" said Barbara, a thirty-eight-year-old mother of two who worked full-time for a pharmaceutical company.

In her own way she was the Lisa of Livingston. By the fall they had enough players for another full team. They arranged to rent an hour on Tuesday nights at the dome, where they would just play each other, week after week, blissfully trapped in the script of *Groundhog Day*. The Livingston Moms against Just for Kicks formed the foundation of what would become a third women's league—one which the likes of Sally Maynard were welcome to try, and to which Phyllis Lowenthal was free to escape.

Recruited into the soccer moms' clinics at temple by Rochelle Sandler, Phyllis was one of the mothers feeling the squeeze, part of the original Sisters of Soccer who were beginning to look more and more like the little sisters of soccer. The team had formed much as

Beth Fuqua's Pokémoms had, but the recruitment of a good player here and a better one there seemed to be an irreversible, self-propelling process. The next thing Phyllis knew, the coach, one of the young players' boyfriends, was bringing in skilled South American women who spoke mostly Spanish on the field to one another. "They were nice girls—one was young enough to be my daughter," Phyllis said. "But I'm forty-seven, a schoolteacher, with two high school kids of my own. What was I doing out there with them?"

She and her teammate Joyce Kosciuszico started to get the hint when their teammates kept calling them by each other's names. They quit the SOS. They found the body language much more to their liking on Tuesday nights. Phyllis enjoyed the instructional hour and jumped at the chance with Sally and the others when the beginners formed a new team to play against the Livingston teams in the winter session. It was Phyllis's third league, from top to middle to bottom, in less than a year, but she had found the level she was comfortable playing at. This was where the original first-foot-forward philosophy was being preserved.

Rather than worry about the eye rolling of her more skilled teammates, Phyllis preferred keeping one out for Sally Maynard. Her children gave her enough experience with people less than half her age. Playing with older women was truly motivational for someone bearing down on fifty. "There just needs to be a place where we don't have to deal with the serious players," she said. "There's a lot more of them, but there's still a lot of us."

Barely more than a year after it all began, and as the new year and the millennium approached, there were fourteen teams and almost two hundred women participating in one of the leagues or the soccer moms' clinics. The train with Lisa and the others had long left the station, but Tuesday was the night to get onboard another, to prove it was never too late. Every week it seemed another newcomer or two would push through the glass doors of the soccer dome, walking bashfully in cleats, looking a little lost, wondering what the hell they were getting themselves into. And one wintry night a woman known to millions across the United States, a veteran star of stage and television screen, fidgeted like a schoolgirl as she awaited the start of her first soccer clinic.

For seventeen years Reva Shayne Lewis had been kicking up a storm on *Guiding Light,* the long-running CBS daytime drama. "I never had time for sports, though," she said when asked if she'd ever done anything athletic on the set besides run after men. "I've been too busy wrecking homes." Wasn't that what the shapers of our entertainment culture believed American women could best relate to? Yet Kim Zimmer, the Emmy-winning actress who played the ravenous Reva, was in fact a car-poolin', SUV-drivin' mother of three, a sports enthusiast and vociferous sideline soccer mom.

Watching her son, Jake, she hardly ever noticed the other teams' mothers doing double takes and whispering, "Is it her?" She loved the game, was dying to try it herself, and finally had to when her husband, the director A. C. Weary, gift-wrapped shorts, shin guards, and cleats, and slipped them under the Christmas tree.

If her first night on the field could have been written into the script, millions of viewers would have finally had a daytime role model, blond and blue-eyed, to motivate them off the couch. As it was, word spread quickly on the Montclair women's soccer grapevine that a popular soap diva was off and kicking, and if Reva should appear limping on an upcoming episode, they would at least know why.

First things first, though: Closer to home, a real-life drama was about to play out. In a suburban town such as Montclair, it didn't take long for the latest dish to spread, especially when the leading lady was involved.

• • •

THE FIRST TIME she walked into the dome, when the news about her marriage was out, when she knew that "they" knew, Lisa was struck by the realization, the most distressing realization, that her life had become a book flipped open to the world. "I went into the dome that first time," she said, "and it was like, 'I don't know if I can deal with this.'"

While she was more self-assured and confident than ever—in part thanks to what she had achieved in soccer—it just wasn't part of Lisa's nature to relish being the center of attention, even for something as positive and benign as her role as organizer, the one "they" still turned to for guidance. "What are the sides?" the others would still sometimes ask her at the most informal scrimmages. "I always want to say, 'I don't have any high seat here,'" she said. "'We're all on par.'" Yet there was no escaping the effort she had made, the sharp perception of who she was. "Lisa Ciardi, founder," some of the television and newspaper features had called her. Every time the women needed to take that next decisive step—to choose up teams, to seek out coaching, to make honest appraisals of ability—it was Lisa, for better or worse, who had made the first move.

Whether she had fancied herself one or not, she was the navigator. She was indisputably the person who deserved to be singled out by Ashley at the anniversary party. Yet Lisa also felt as if she had been walking a fine line, between an almost proprietary responsibility for the group and her own self-interest and the competitive needs that motivated her in the first place. "It's a lot of pressure, you know?" she said.

That, it turned out, was nothing compared to what came now, her most difficult balancing act, the sidestepping of her local celebrity to maintain a low personal profile as she entered the minefield of divorce. Too late, she intuitively knew, as she pushed through the revolving doors to walk onto the field, where, she believed and feared, "all eyes were on me."

It hadn't been long into the year that word had spread, the way it usually does—in whispered playground conversations, in late-night telephone chats—that Lisa and Brian Ciardi had split up. Lord knows they weren't the first in town. In fact, Lisa wasn't even the first of the soccer-playing mothers whose marriage had ended or teetered. But she was not just one of the gang. Lisa was Madame Soccer Mom.

Maybe the others weren't as determined or talented, but Lisa had set a standard of commitment. To a certain extent, favorably or not, many of the others measured themselves against her. Now came the news of Lisa's marital breakup, with the eyebrow-raising addendum that she was seeing Kevin McGrath, the fairly new—and obviously younger—soccer trainer from Liverpool. Beyond the culturally ingrained need to gossip, the human temptation to reduce something as complex and private as a withering marriage into a tabloid headline, this dramatic turn was sure to provoke a heated response. The temptation was too great to react reflexively, to wonder if she had simply taken soccer too far.

Brian Ciardi, understandably, believed so. Soccer was just a game, he said shortly after their breakup. How could sports have intruded so powerfully, so negatively, in his family life? Sport was not life. As much as he loved hockey, as great a boost to his self-image and esteem as it was when he'd played in college, he had come to accept the fact more than twenty years ago that it could never be more than a hobby, a diversion. A night out he enjoyed to work off the midlife stresses of family and work.

"The soccer thing got out of control," he said. "I could see it happening as the months went on, things that weren't getting done because of soccer. Lisa let herself become defined by it." Of course, it was much easier to put sports—or any new passion, for that matter—into that broader perspective when it was old hat, when one had had the opportunity to participate for half a lifetime, as opposed to a year.

It was fairly obvious to those who had watched Lisa almost single-handedly build the foundation of interest that she was in determined pursuit of the outlet, deeply invested in the cause. At least it was obvious to Ashley. "This is something entirely different for Lisa than it is for most of the others," he had said months earlier. "You could see that from the beginning."

Yet it was also too simplistic, almost insultingly so, to suggest that it was a love for this game or any game that was at the root of Lisa's resolve to make such dramatic changes in her life. "Soccer was a conduit," Brian admitted, and what he meant was that it had been an escape hatch from more conventional and often suffocating problems for the modern couple: The grueling commutes. The marathon workweeks that are not supposed to last beyond long-attained promotions and financial objectives. The days without significant time together that turn into weeks. The tendency to live through the kids, and the unrelenting and ultimately unfulfilling quest for a bigger house and more comfort that you one day realize may not be very comfortable at all.

By many standards, and by those some in Montclair would inevitably use to judge her, Lisa already had it all—a smart and successful husband, three beautiful and healthy children, a fabulous home, and a place in an enviable town. But security and stability were not the qualities that made Lisa so successful in her effort to launch the women's soccer movement; it was her resourcefulness, her energy, her refusal to be defined by age and place, qualities that had captured the attention of the young, idealistic yet intuitive Camilla Bertelsen. Why, as Camilla had asked after her nights out with the mothers at Tierney's, did people have to suppress or lose those qualities after a certain age, after bearing children, after "settling down"?

Soccer, you might say, roused Lisa from the American suburban dream. It was anything but a comfort zone, the way she drove herself to create it and took responsibility for its failure or success. It was comparable to what her mother had done at age thirty-seven—gone back to school, embarked on a new career. In terms of energy and effort, it was as if Lisa had started her own business, the one exception being that she wasn't reaping rewards. Not financial rewards, anyway.

But if she was defining herself by or devoting too much time to her "work," then how different was she from the majority of the working population? "I could have started a number of things," Lisa said. "Something, anything, that would have helped me feel like a more complete person on the inside and helped me make decisions about my life." She had felt the need, viscerally at least, to do it for herself, to give herself something more.

"The whole idea of the women playing together in a team sport, the cohesiveness, the closeness, probably helped me to become a more whole person, a more independent person, altered my personality a bit, how I feel about myself," Lisa said. "It may have made me a stronger person on the inside, and maybe because I did spearhead it and get it rolling, and it did turn out so well, it made me feel that I could do other things for myself.

"I began to like the side of me that's become very aggressive and focused and that helped me lay it out on the line. Maybe that's courage, but soccer in itself didn't make decisions for me."

The truth was that only those she was closest to could possibly know what had. "People like Clare knew something was up, but with the team I was very private about everything," Lisa said. "It seemed that our whole team had gone through stuff." Venera had had the war in Kosovo to deal with, and not long after that, her father-in-law grew gravely ill. Jeanne Jeffrey's mother was ailing with cancer, only months after Jeanne's father had died.

"I didn't feel that the team was there for me to verbally unload on," Lisa said. "Soccer was more of an outlet to relieve the tension and stress I'd been feeling for months. But even though I didn't see the team as a place to unburden myself that much, I knew they were there for me, all of them. I'd always had friends I could confide in, but there was something special about your teammates just accepting you for who you are, for your place on the field. So you just put everything aside for a couple of hours, feel as if things are normal, and go play."

She realized that she was going to be a conversation piece for a few weeks, maybe longer, because Montclair was "a small town and you have no choice, and everyone, I guess, is entitled to an opinion." What she didn't appreciate, though, was the "chatter" she'd been hearing, a few of the husbands not portraying Ashley's trainers in the fondest way, or at least becoming less than sanguine about the soccer social scene, the regular mixing of married mothers with younger men and women. "It's like being back in college," one husband said, "except most of these women have children waiting for them back at home."

In its most extreme form this perception was accurate, and would have been for either parent. But it was important to keep in mind that for generations men had been finding opportunities to mix with younger women, to the point where doing so was considered a stereotype. Whatever the social explications were, Lisa didn't appreciate her very personal situation being cast in any mold, or the trainers taking the blame for her private choices. "Stupid men's talk," she called it—reactionary thinking that completely dismissed all the good the women's soccer movement had done in town, all the relationships and family units that undoubtedly had been strengthened by it.

Beth and Tom Panucci, for example, liked to clear the living room furniture aside to practice their soccer footwork when their girls were asleep. Ed Martoglio wound up on crutches, with a torn ligament in his knee, after his first coed game with Barbara; when he decided that was enough for him, Barbara recruited her ten-year-old, Richard, and Friday became mother and son's regular night out. Ed did coach his girls, though, with Barbara alongside him. The Wrights, Cathy and Ian, became co-coaches of their daughter's and son's teams. Beth Fuqua coached first-grade soccer with her husband, Howard Kerbel, and Beth Albert. She became the league commissioner and conscience, cautioning the ever-eager dads against putting too great an emphasis on winning. When one of the first-grade players was asked to choose a special person in his life for his school's "Heroes Fair," little Sam Obaditch picked the two Beths. At the event they were summoned to the stage with the other heroes, almost all men. Sam read his poem, "An Ode to Beth and Beth": "They teach us to be a good sport, don't be mean, let the other team feel happy because it's not a dream . . ."

They were role models in the community, and at home with their children and, in some cases, their husbands. "It's been great with both of us coaching and, frankly, Beth knew more of the how-to aspects of it than I did," Howard Kerbel said. "She ran practices, which I don't think I could have done. I didn't play soccer."

He didn't play sports as a child because he was born with a congenital heart defect, a hole between the ventricles. By the time it was corrected, he was ten and gun-shy. "I was the scorekeeper at the swim meets, things like that," he said. "So in a way Beth's playing soccer has allowed me to live the experience of trying team sports for the first time through her, through the stories. As she's enjoyed it, I've enjoyed it. When she's been hurt and enjoyed it less, then I've enjoyed it less. But I've always been supportive because I could see what it meant to her. When she got hurt, we dealt with it. It forced me to get home from work at a decent hour and, in a way, stay in touch with my priorities, too."

He tried a soccer clinic for men, thought it was fun, but didn't stay with it. The men in the group had all played one sport or another already; they were just getting exercise, or out of the house. "What made it so different and good for the women was that so many of them were doing something for the first time and doing it together," he said. "They developed a love for this particular game."

Not every husband dropped into the dome for a game here and there. Nina Sloan made a point of saying that her husband had showed little interest in her new life in the net. Then again, there weren't many women watching the men play in the dome either. And there were, of course, other ways of demonstrating support, starting with being home to take care of the kids, with respecting a woman's right to have the same outlets as men.

Rochelle Sandler's husband, Joe Campeas, a rabid fan of many team sports, made no bones about the fact that soccer wasn't one of them. He admitted it was a game he couldn't watch unless his kids and now Rochelle were playing it. But he was tickled that she was playing, getting out and in shape, and that his fourth- and second-grade boys, Danny and Sammy, would invariably ask Rochelle, never him, to kick the ball around the backyard.

Joe's passion was baseball, and his longtime hobby was tracking famous athletes and obtaining their autographs on the *Sports Illustrated* covers he religiously collected. He traveled for his work and made a point of knowing where the pro teams in a city were staying. He could talk his way past the FBI, and once, when they were traveling together, Joe told Rochelle to wait while he made a call in the lobby of their hotel; within minutes David Wells, then with the Yankees, appeared to shoot the breeze. That same season Joe somehow talked the reigning Yankees matinee idol, Derek Jeter, into calling Rochelle's daughter, Becky.

Then there was the night, several years past, when the phone rang—Joe calling from somewhere on the road, in a bar. "Hold on," he said. "Someone wants to say hello."

"How ya'll doooin'?" Mickey Mantle drawled.

So one day, when the U.S. Women's World Cup team was in New Jersey on its indoor tour, Joe called the hotel and asked for Brandi Chastain. He told her about his wife, about the Pokémoms and all the mothers in Montclair. He asked if he might send her a couple of items to sign. Not long after, Rochelle received a copy of the July 19, 1999, issue of *Sports Illustrated,* the one with the shirtless Chastain celebrating her winning shoot-out goal. "To Rochelle," she wrote. "Thank you for believing that soccer is for everyone to enjoy. Best of luck on the field. I'm proud of you." Signed, Brandi Chastain. Rochelle was the envy of all the night she brought the framed cover to the dome; the others gathered round like a bunch of starstruck kids.

What a shame, thought Lisa, that of all places in the community, and she of all people, should feel so uncomfortable, so nervous, just coming through the front door. Yet that first time back after the news of her marital breakup was out, she also realized she had no choice. People could think whatever they were going to think. She was going forward, going through the door, because the only alternative was to walk away, to become a spectator again. She knew that was not going to happen.

"Just going into the dome that first time was so hard," she said. "I knew a lot of it was going around, but then what actually happened made me feel amazed, touched, relieved. People I didn't really know—not like Clare and Dana, just women I played some soccer with—would walk up and say, 'Whatever you need, I support you and your decision, and if this is good for you, if you're happy, then that's great.'

"I was really shocked with that. They would just come up and say these things and give me a hug, and it was just to let me know that they were thinking about me. I was very relieved that people really didn't care, or at least they didn't act like they did. It didn't matter. It wasn't like I'd changed."

Far more than most, Meg could understand what she meant, for she had been there herself, albeit under different conditions and much less publicly. Meg was the one who could promise Lisa that the rawness of the situation would fade, that lives would carry on, that the young ones could and eventually would adjust. A woman who had been divorced with three young children, who had married a younger man, a soccer coach, could speak from experience. She could assure Lisa that these choices were her choices and ultimately only for her and her loved ones to be concerned with. Meg could share stories, including one of a recent communion that best illustrated how the broken halves of a once-unified family managed to coexist for the sake of the child.

"She approached me and told me those stories, which made it so much easier," Lisa said. "She's very honest, frank about her own situation, generous to share it with me. It took a lot of courage for her, because it could have been awkward, or maybe I wouldn't want to talk."

Not all that long ago, *unapproachable* was exactly the opinion Meg had of Lisa, and Lisa had reacted in kind. The dome had not been big enough for both of them, but if soccer had matched them as adversaries on opposite sides of the Belles–Badgers divide, it had also allowed them to build a bridge across it. Now these competitive women of uncommon resilience had more to talk about than they'd ever dreamed possible.

"It was bad enough the way we all acted, like a bunch of goofs, but our kids were all here," Meg said. "I just think there were a lot of insecurities out there. And Lisa, to me, seemed very intense, not real warm. It took me a long time to realize that she's also very quiet, easy to misread." Now Meg read Lisa loud and clear, and wanted very much to share what she knew. Now Lisa found Meg comforting and caring, and she relished every word.

•   •   •

E VEN LIFETIME blew the story of how dedicated these women were, and how much they were willing to sacrifice to play the game. The producers from the women's cable network had come to Montclair looking for a team that represented the true all-moms' spirit. For several weeks, from late fall through midwinter, the Poké-moms were quickly becoming a triumph of that spirit, going 2–2–2 during a six-game stretch.

They were getting contributions and goals from all different sources. In a 5–0 victory over the Flash, Rochelle stunned everyone, including herself, by scoring a hat trick, positioning herself smartly in front of the net and using her strong right foot. It was another example of what Filip had been preaching—talent-wise, maybe they wouldn't improve all that much individually, but they could be clearly better at playing as a team. They had figured out their natural positions. They were more inclined to respond to game conditions without worrying that they were trying too hard to win. What the hell, it felt good, damn good, when they beat the Flash twice, tied the Beanie Babes and then the Chicks with Cleats.

One late January night, with Nina in goal and Beth Panucci on defense for the entire game, they played the SOS to a scoreless standstill until Barrie Schwartz got a fortunate bounce near the net for the game's only goal. One–nothing to the SOS! What might they be capable of next?

Unfortunately, the lack of defining parameters for the intermediate league soon raised the odds once again. Field time was scarce in the dome in general, and for the open league in particular. Players good enough for the higher level who were locked out began pushing down into the intermediate league, which by this point needed an over-thirty or over-thirty-five limit. By April, the beginning of spring league, it had become younger again, only one or two players a team, but enough to make the games more daunting, and on some nights downright depressing. A whole new team of younger women, calling itself the Bomb, had joined. The sight of "Pokémoms versus Bomb" on the schedule had explosive incongruity written all over it.

At least the Pokémoms could brag that, excluding the beginner league and Rilee McDonald, they were the last full team of mothers. That distinction earned them their very own feature on the Lifetime news show after Ashley made the referral. The crew descended on the Pokémoms' practice one April Sunday, interviewing Cathy, Rochelle, Diane Gray, and the captain, Beth Fuqua.

"It's a physical game," Beth said, smiling into the camera. "But we have kids and jobs and husbands who travel, and we can't afford to have a sprained ankle for six weeks." Nor a broken arm, which Beth would sadly and ironically suffer the following night, as the cameras rolled.

The Pokémoms were losing 2–1 early in the second half to the Chicks, Beth taking a turn in goal, when a hard shot was lifted from the middle, to her left. Up went her arm, the hand not clenched, as it should have been. The ball crashed off her wrist into the corner of the net. She knew it was bad right away, grabbing it with her right hand, screaming out, bending over in agony and . . .

Cut to a smiling anchor in the studio, concluding another feel-good segment with the sugary chant "You go, girl." The only place Beth went was to the hospital, where her left arm was diagnosed as broken.

She would admit that she hadn't exactly encouraged the crew to document her latest and most painful injury. Although the reporter followed up with a call, no mention of her misfortune was made in the feature that ultimately ran. Nothing about the vexing trilogy of injuries Beth had suffered, from the very first ankle turn in the park, through being slide-tackled in the dome, to winding up with the worst break of all the original players, her left arm in a raised cast for weeks. Nothing about the trade-offs, the risks as well as the rewards, the ongoing debate of how hard a mother should play, and against whom.

Even Lisa, of all people, was beginning to wonder. By the end of the winter season, the Madness had added several new players, as Jen and Caroline took the challenge to organize better and rounded up a youthful posse. They were soon in first place, and began the last night needing only to avoid losing to the second-place Xtreme by fewer than nine goals.

For a while it looked as if the Xtreme just might pull it off as they built a 4–1 lead. The tension began to get thick. But then came the second half, when even Sarah Hogan couldn't prevent a barrage of Madness goals, when Lisa's core mothers for the first time looked outclassed, fallible, and fatigued. "I feel so old," Jeanne Jeffrey said, coming off the field after the 7–5 victory gave the Madness the title, and Jen and Caroline their measure of revenge.

By the spring season even more former college players were streaming into the league. The Badgers upgraded with several new faces. Lisa kept an eye out for help, but her team struggled, and for the first time it slipped out of contention for first place. The old gang didn't seem the same. Dana was busy with work and missed many games. Jeanne and Clare wondered if they belonged anymore. "A lot of the older women on my team are afraid of getting injured because of the level of play," Lisa said, echoing Beth Fuqua from almost a year before. "We're in a funny position, maybe between the two leagues."

The proprietor in her was ready to roll up her sleeves and get back to work, figure out the next step in this rapid evolution. Lisa's life was in deep transition, though; she was moving soon with the kids, to another house in town, and she was exploring a return to the workforce.

Soccer had a big place in her new life. But it wasn't her whole life. "I'd still love to revamp things, modify what's going on," she said. "Even if it's balanced, a lot of the women are going to get bored playing the same women, the same teams. I have ideas on how to improve the program, maybe merge it with the women from New York, form teams that could play outdoors, eleven versus eleven, travel every once in a while, and play in tournaments. I just don't know if I have the time right now, the energy I had when this all began, to put into it."

Then came a call from a woman whose energy seemed limitless, an offer from another leading lady that Lisa and the others couldn't refuse.

13

Rainy Day Women

F OR EIGHTEEN MONTHS she had saved these bills, collected on a soccer pitch and presented to her caked with dirt
and sweat, then stuffed into a small white envelope—the
wrinkled benefaction of the young and hardly affluent women from
the Bronx Irish League. Wendy Hollender pulled the thick wad of
cash from the envelope and proudly raised it high for her audience to
see. "Now they're all neatly pressed from sitting in the bottom of my
drawer," she said. "You might say, they're all dressed up and ready for
this special occasion."

Decked out in a black jacket and matching pants, color-coordi-
nated with her fully regrown entanglement of curls, Wendy looked
up inside the small amphitheater to the crowd that included the people she loved most: her family members, her closest teammates, and
her friends from the Parlour Moms. Bless them all, for pushing

through the Friday rush-hour traffic on this raw spring evening, fo
navigating the winding back roads on the campus of Montclair Stat
University, for being there, as always, when she needed them.

She had so much to share, in so little time. There were other
alongside her, medical dignitaries and sports semicelebrities, blink
ing into the stage lights before a crowd of about seventy-five—whic
might have been larger if there'd been better weather and more tim
to plan. It was still amazing and wonderful, Wendy thought, what
few determined women from opposite sides of the Hudson Rive
could put together in only a handful of weeks, how they'd banded a
one, become a team. Teamwork 2000, they called this benefit fo
breast cancer awareness, a symposium and companion soccer tour
nament that began with a telephone call, an invitation from Wend
to the Montclair women to join her in playing for a cause, a goal,
vision. Wendy's vision.

In her experiences with cancer support groups at Mount Sina
Hospital, she grew increasingly saddened at how demoralized s
many of the women became, and how withdrawn from even th
simplest of daily routines. She had been fortunate, she knev
Blessed. She wished they all could have the kind of support, spiritu
and physical, the Parlour Moms had provided her.

"Imagine a program run by volunteers, women who have ha
breast cancer," she wrote in what would become an integral part c
Teamwork 2000's promotional pitch. "Buddies to take you out for
walk, a run, and later, for aerobics. They encourage you when yo
don't want to get out of bed during chemo. They put on music fc
you when you work out. They watch your kids. They keep track c
your improvement. There could be a team, with a coach, a mor
experienced survivor, that would set goals and celebrate achievin
them." At the very beginning, before she'd understood the resourc
and the enthusiasm that were available to her in Montclair, all Wend

had done was imagine. Now, suddenly, she had a team, a plan, and a place where it could all unfold.

Upon hearing of Wendy's idea and her search for a facility, Beth Albert telephoned her friend David Kaplan, director of the Yogi Berra Museum and Learning Center. Only eighteen months old—and best known as the place where the Yankees' owner, George Steinbrenner, had begged the forgiveness of the catching legend to end their fourteen-year feud—the museum had quickly become a local hotbed of athletic and educational activity.

Built with private funds, the museum was nestled into a corner of the university campus, along with the adjacent Berra Stadium, which housed an independent minor-league team. Kaplan, a former newspaper editor, was more interested in serious issues than he was in using the facility for card shows and other aggrandizing events. The museum board included Suzyn Waldman, the local sports radio personality who had convinced Steinbrenner to pay Berra the visit in January 1999. Waldman happened to be a breast cancer survivor.

Kaplan contacted the university's athletic director—a woman, luckily enough. Holly Gera invited them all to a meeting, to which she came equipped with an offer: They could have the school's soccer fields on Saturday, May 20. With that the symposium date was set for May 19, and Teamwork was in business.

Wendy recruited Maggie Bradley-Cook and Joan Madden-Peister, among others, to work with her, to make the weekly planning runs from Manhattan to Montclair. Beth Albert became the public relations liaison. Beth Fuqua dug out source and donation lists she had compiled from previous charity work. Cathy Wright lent her artistic talents and connections for the development of logos and T-shirts. Lisa hit the poster-hanging trail again and organized one of the two Montclair teams that would play in the four-team women's tournament (a four-team girls' tournament was added to raise youth awareness). Ashley provided his group insurance policy against injury in the tournament for the Montclair women at a nominal cost.

Barbara Martoglio showed up one day with a box of certificates for free mammograms—courtesy of the Montclair Breast Center—and in time they were distributed to the younger players who didn't have health care. Maggie handed Wendy a check from Joseph Lelyveld, executive editor for *The New York Times* and Maggie's physical therapy client. They tapped professional contacts for help, for possible symposium panelists. They made brash and personal pleas.

A well-known breast cancer specialist from St. Barnabas Hospital in nearby Livingston, Richard A. Michaelson, agreed to attend the symposium. Wendy lined up a Mount Sinai contact, Roberta Levy Schwartz, who had been stricken at the unthinkable age of twenty-seven, and founded a group called the Young Survival Coalition. Dave Kaplan tapped into the motivational speaker network and lined up RuthAnn Lobo, mother of the women's basketball star Rebecca, and a survivor and author.

If only they could get a soccer player, Wendy thought. Wouldn't that be a kick? On Parlour Moms' stationery she authored a heartfelt invitation to the World Cup star Michelle Akers in Oviedo, Florida. They had met briefly at a Women's Sports Foundation dinner the previous fall. Little Wendy told lanky Michelle, who had persevered for a couple of years through various ailments, how much of an inspiration she had been as Wendy had fought cancer. Michelle mentioned that her father was undergoing chemotherapy, so she could more than imagine how difficult it was.

Michelle wrote back, saying she wished she could attend but could not. A call was placed to Sue Rodin, the agent for Julie Foudy, the team's de facto ambassador. Foudy, who lived on the West Coast, could not travel that distance for one night. Rodin had a suggestion, though: Saskia Webber was no household name, no icon in cleats, but she had been the World Cup backup goalie to Briana Scurry. In women's soccer circles she was an established commodity. Better yet, she was local, more likely to come.

Raised in Princeton, Saskia was a four-year starter at Rutgers from 1989 through 1992, had played three professional seasons in Japan, and had produced five victories and a tie in six starts with the national team. Now she was on soccer sabbatical, awaiting the planned pro league in the States being formed for spring 2001. The product of a mixed-race marriage, Saskia was a most exotic Jersey girl: light-skinned black, tall and proportionally muscular, drop-dead gorgeous, and in the current employ of Wilhelmina Models.

Beyond her sharing of the team's dirty little dietary secrets—how Foudy, for instance, made sure every training table was stocked with cookies—Saskia, though not yet thirty, made it plain when she stood to speak that she was hardly unenlightened on the subject of breast cancer. She recalled the awful day the telephone rang while she was playing in Japan, and her mother broke the news that doctors had found a lump in her breast. "Luckily, it was benign," she said. "But I remember holding my breath every day until we found out. And I think that's when I lost the youthful sense of invulnerability."

More than most, elite athletes in their prime have to cling to the belief that their bodies won't betray them. As she trained during the spring of 1999 for the most heralded women's team sports competition in American history, Saskia felt soreness in her lower breast. For several days she pushed off the awful possibilities. She just hoped the ache would go away, but when it persisted, she began to worry. She thought of her mother, and of a childhood friend who had been stricken as a young adult.

"I've got to go see my gynecologist in Princeton," Saskia recalled telling her coach, Tony DiCicco. She left the team. "Literally right before the opening game," she said.

The soreness, fortunately, turned out to be nothing more than a muscle strain. Saskia rejoined her team in time for the opening ceremonies at Giants Stadium—the same way Wendy, within months, would rush back to the Parlour Moms just days after being under the knife.

That chilly May night, on a small stage with the backdrop of a model scoreboard from the old Yankee Stadium, Wendy spoke of her bad days and better days. How soccer had kept her moving, zigzagging her way forward, like a child navigating his or her way around orange cones. In the audience her family beamed, and several of her teammates nodded because, perhaps even more than her blood relatives, they knew the level of Wendy's commitment and courage, and what she had achieved in the previous months.

A soccer player could best understand how hard it had been to just keep going. "To win a World Cup pales in comparison," Saskia would say, turning and looking straight at Wendy. "You won your life."

In the glare of the lights, Wendy's eyes moistened and she blushed, not the reaction those who best knew her said they'd have expected from this most focused and headstrong woman. But this wasn't a relative or friend, a teammate or even a physician, telling her how remarkable she was. Saskia Webber was a World Cup veteran, a veritable goddess dressed in pink blouse, blue jeans, and black boots, hair tied back, as she towered over surgically scarred and repaired Wendy. And she was telling her: "I am humbled to be here with you."

Who in the audience could not say the same words when Wendy held up that stack of bills collected by those young women, many of them immigrants who had no health insurance of their own but whose old country's custom demanded they help? What mother in the audience, or anywhere from Manhattan to Montclair, could have resisted a knowing smile as Wendy told of how she was often tempted to dig for that stash when she "needed quick cash for the kids for lunch money, or whatever."

She never touched it, though. "I was saving it for a special occasion," she said. Another day.

A rainy day.

E VEN BY SEATTLE'S soggiest standards, Saturday, May 20, 2000, was a cruel joke for nature to play on northern New Jersey so late in the spring. At the end of a long, wet week, despite forecasts that had raised hopes for relief, the rain was still falling persistently enough to defy the brief intervals of brightening sky. It soon became apparent that the sun wasn't going to shine on this day, and as if the rain wasn't enough to contend with, there was also the matter of the fifty-something-degree temperature. The bone-rattling chill made joints moan arthritically and waterlogged clothes feel like those X-ray jackets they put over your chest in the dentist's chair.

By 8:00 A.M., with the tournament due to begin at 10:00, Holly Gera had notified Dave Kaplan that the Montclair State grass field would not be available because of its lack of proper drainage. She suggested that the women's and under-sixteen girls' tournaments be played on artificial turf in the stadium that was used for football and soccer. That meant all the games would be on short-sided fields, eight versus eight.

The Montclair women were especially disappointed; they had rarely played full-field soccer, eleven versus eleven, and they were intrigued by the chance to play with the offside rule, which they had been practicing under the tutelage of Eileen Blair, the Montclair State women's coach. The change in plans also meant that the Poké-moms would be overstocked with players, because they had expanded their roster with friends from Chicks with Cleats to include more local women in the benefit.

One of them, Joyce Milano, had been a beneficiary of the soccer moms' first stab at philanthropy several months before, not long after she had moved to Montclair to live with a local family and help care for a young autistic boy. Joyce was from Kenya, a thirty-eight-year-old single woman who had been in the United States for almost a decade, teaching preschool while completing studies for a career in special education with a concentration in autism. As a teenager in Nairobi, she had briefly played recreational soccer with her brothers, and watching the Women's World Cup final shortly after she arrived in Montclair reminded her how much she loved it. One afternoon the daughter in the home in which she was living returned from Ashley's Soccer Camp and mentioned there was a mothers' group at the camp. Joyce inquired and was in the dome, on a team, by early fall.

Then came distressing news from home—her thirty-four-year-old sister, Cathy, the mother of a seven-year-old daughter, was suffering from a rare brain tumor. She would need surgery, in England, that would cost thousands in U.S. dollars her family did not have. By the time the women in her new community were finished, Joyce had a five-thousand-dollar check to send home; her father borrowed the rest, and her sister had the surgery.

A woman who wanted to spend her working life helping the neediest kind of child felt as if she had found a place where she might live, work, and play for a very long time. "At this stage of my life, I was just thrilled to have a chance to play soccer again," Joyce said. "But what really struck me about being in this community was that I could do something I always loved and do it with women who seemed so eager to use it not only to compete and have fun but to enhance someone's well-being."

She leapt at the chance to play for the cause of breast cancer, regardless of the soggy and scaled-down day. A semipro game between a team from New Hampshire and one from New Jersey was canceled, as were plans to have booths set up with breast cancer literature, the on-site facility for free breast checkups, and other assorted fund-raising efforts for Teamwork 2000. The concession stands would not open. Gone was the anticipation of playing before a crowd, even one composed predominantly of the players' families.

But was all that so bad? As Cathy Wright rationalized, wasn't soccer supposed to be a metaphor here? Wasn't this a perfect day for all of them to play and persevere through the storm clouds and the bad hand nature too often dealt?

Cathy's mother, now eighty-seven and suffering from Alzheimer's back in Philadelphia, had set that example for her daughter three and a half decades ago—when breast cancer was less a public scourge and more a woman's private hell. Elizabeth LeCleire's response to breast cancer and a double mastectomy was to build a swimming pool and buy the most fashionable bathing suit she could find: to state, in no uncertain terms, that she—and no one else—would define what Cathy called "her own sense of femininity."

Cathy had run marathons in worse weather than this. Soccer was like that; barring thunder and lightning, the game always went on.

So although one of the four girls teams failed to show, the two women's teams from Montclair and the two from New York came rolling into the parking lot right on schedule. The women smiled sheepishly at each other and defiantly at the rain and at the wonderful craziness of it all. They wore funky gear. They clomped through puddles. They lugged coolers into the locker room.

Hell, yes, they were playing, and they all had their reasons, some more personal than others. Cathy's mother had survived breast cancer. A close friend of Ellen Paretti's had not. And, as Beth Fuqua said, soccer was very much a recreational primer on the "lessons of life." The way she looked at it, it was a game above all, but one "where if something bad happens, you just try to keep going."

If anyone had a good reason to stop, it was Beth; she had three reasons, actually, each injury more serious than the last. The cast for her broken left arm unceremoniously captured on film by Lifetime was only days removed. She hardly needed the inclement weather to discourage her from playing. Had she asked for permission, her doctor would have told her to forget it, play it safe, avoid the elbow throwers and slide tacklers. As the weakest of the four teams, the Pokémoms were surely in for a few one-sided beatings.

Did Beth really need to do this? "I feel like I should at least try," she said. She didn't care how much she played, or if her team even scored a goal; she wanted to be a part of the occasion, felt she ought to be, just as Jeanne Jeffrey was present and accounted for only days after having lost her mother. That made two parents lost to cancer in less than a year.

To someone in her state of mind, Jeanne quietly confided, the chilly rain actually felt pretty damn good.

A S THE XTREME gathered for the tournament kickoff against the Parlour Moms, Ravan Magrath unveiled her multicolored Ramapo College goalie jersey, Number 12, and was immediately set upon by Vanessa Hardwick. "So, Ravan," Vanessa said, poking fun. "Are you going to be a lunatic today?"

"Not today," Ravan said. "No way." She looked down at her feet, then kneeled to lace her cleats. "My mother died of breast cancer, you know."

Most of the women she had played against still didn't know. Lisa, of course, did, and had made the caring gesture, inviting Ravan to join Meg and Minnie and a few other Badgers on her team.

The truth was that Ravan had come a long way in one year, from back when she was the original scourge of the women's soccer movement. For one thing, the open league was much younger and more aggressive now, making Ravan less of an anomaly. For another, it became obvious to many of the women as the months passed that she really meant no harm. She was usually sorry for her outbursts. She always promised to try harder. She could take Vanessa's and anyone else's good-natured ribbing. It was obvious by now that Ravan had heart, and had grown on many of these mothers, like some impudent kid sister who occasionally had to be put in her place.

Actually, the Badgers had already positioned Ravan in the perfect place—in goal, her regular perch now, where she could talk a blue streak and throw herself about, harassing only the ball. Sarah Hogan, the Xtreme's regular goalie, was injured and unavailable for the tournament, so Ravan would be in the net for the whole day. She learned this from Vanessa, who would be coaching these games as if her Football Association license depended on winning them.

Victory, not surprisingly, was Lisa's mandate. She loved the idea of playing for a cause, especially this cause, but she also relished the challenge, the opportunity to play against the Parlour Moms one year after their getting-to-know-you scrimmage in the park. This was just what she'd been seeking, an outlet beyond the sameness of the dome games. She had carefully picked her team, sending out personalized invitations. And while the Xtreme were still playing in their withered gray T-shirts back in the dome, Lisa had new shirts with a red and black design specially made for this big day.

She didn't kid herself: The original soccer moms' spirit had been diluted. Even Lisa usually stayed back on defense now. The twenty-something women were the goal scorers, the stars of her team. But Lisa didn't care about that. She could clearly see the difference in skill levels now, where these young girls were coming from and where she would not be going. Competing against the likes of a former high school player like Jen McEwan was one thing; one of her team's recent additions, Martha Kraeger, was not long removed from the Division I college program at Holy Cross. Another new player was barely out of high school. It was becoming obvious that, sooner or later, Lisa would have to address the same issues Barbara and Ellen and some of the others already had. For now, though, Lisa had a tournament to play and win.

Even with Karen Sherris, the Ashley's Soccer Camp coach who had trained the Bluestone Belles, in uniform and ready to go, it was a stretch to suggest that Lisa had shown up with ringers. This was never intended to be a soccer moms' clinic. In order to compete in the Bronx Irish League, the Parlour Moms themselves had made the same concession to youth several years ago.

Over the years women would hear of the Parlour Moms from one source or another. They would call, asking to play, but there was no clinic or beginner league for Wendy to direct them to, as there was in Montclair, and the Parlour Moms' level was too advanced. So Wendy kept a list and eventually, when she had enough names, put them all in touch.

Wendy agreed that the Velocity, the team subsequently formed featuring the young actress Julia Stiles and her mother, Judith, might have been a better fit for this tournament. She couldn't help it, though: She had a soft spot for the Harps who had an entire roster of players under thirty. They were the kinds of "outer-borough" young women who had participated in the "Potato Famine" collection for her. A few of them had accompanied the Parlour Moms to Ireland the previous summer, drunk with them in the pubs, and celebrated after Wendy's three goals won the last game.

It soon became clear that the Harps were likely to keep the Parlour Moms from reaching the championship game, following a round-robin format. The Xtreme didn't dominate the Parlour Moms in the first game but took an early lead on Kris Smith's header on the way to a comfortable 3–1 decision. Then the Harps routed the Pokémoms. The third game, a preview of the final, was a fierce struggle between the Xtreme and the Harps, with a late Xtreme goal salvaging a 1–1 tie.

The Parlour Moms won a 3–1 decision over the Pokémoms,

who appreciated how the Manhattan women rested their younger players, making for a more competitive match. In their final game the Parlour Moms came close to rearranging the championship seeding, with Wendy buzzing around the net in the closing minutes of a 1–1 game. After twice narrowly missing the left post, she admitted how much she had wanted to score on this of all days. But the game ended 1–1, and the tournament was over for the Parlour Moms, barring a miracle: a Pokémoms defeat of the Xtreme. "The Pokémoms aren't going to beat them," one of the Harps complained on the sideline, impatient at having to wait out another game before playing the final. "Why can't they play after the championship game?" said another.

Beyond the formality of qualification, the answer had something to do with the fact that the Pokémoms had also been out there, all day, in the rain. And it had everything to do with the proposition the older women had championed: They all deserved their time, their games, regardless of size and speed and skill. On top of that, many of these Pokémoms could tell the Harps of a game they had played, once upon a time, when their goalie was red-carded and they played a woman down and . . .

Poof. There would be no miracle victory or tie this time around. The Xtreme scored early and often. They won by eight goals.

Yet as predictably one-sided as the game was, the Pokémoms did score, and Beth Albert did tackle Karen Sherris in the open field during the second half, relieving the fancy-footed trainer of the ball as she dribbled about, Harlem Globetrotter style. Players on the sidelines from both teams roared their approval. Karen shrugged and raised her arms in mock surrender; Beth raised hers in triumph. It was a shining moment if ever there was one. "These women are amazing," said Eileen Blair, the university's women's coach, on the sideline. "Just amazing."

She had grown up in "Soccer Town," Kearny, where she had

known Jen McEwan and Connie Meola and all the rest. Fairly new to the Montclair community, she had heard about these soccer moms and loved the idea of older women playing the game. To see them first-hand, she said, was a treat in itself. "I'd love to coach them," she said. "They enjoy it so much, no matter what the score is."

Could winning and losing be defined, under these circum-stances, by wins and losses? Though the Parlour Moms had only one more victory than the Pokémoms to show for their afternoon in the rain, Wendy and Maggie sure felt like champions, huddled under an umbrella watching their daughters, Abby and Julia, win the under-sixteen tournament with their team, the Manhattan Devils. "Which one is yours?" one of the Montclair women would walk by and ask. In those moments, proud as they were wet, Wendy felt like the luck-iest mother of all.

Someone like Lisa could do the instant math: By the time she was Wendy's age, in another half-dozen years, her own second-grade daughter would be roughly the same age as Abby. Maybe they would be lucky enough to share such a day, experience the high of taking turns, of mother pulling for daughter and daughter rooting for mom. "You see these things and hear these stories," Lisa said, "and you keep realizing there are so many things to get out of this, so many ways to enjoy it."

Of course Wendy, like Lisa, played to win, probably more than most. Yet once again, as it had in Ireland, soccer provided her with a much greater prize, a stirring appreciation of all she had and desper-ately wished to hold on to. The best soccer moments weren't always between the lines. Wendy would never forget the smell of those lush Irish fields, the sound of laughter in the pubs. And now, the crowd-ing around the blow dryers in the Montclair State locker rooms and the encounters with the gang of ponytailed girls.

"Do you know why we had this event?" Beth Albert asked the

group from Queens between matches, the teenagers picking at the mothers' snacks. It surprised her when they shrugged. No one, apparently, had explained what the pink ribbons on the women's shirts represented. Nobody had told them about the cardboard donation boxes or the gray T-shirts with the striking Teamwork 2000 logo for each of them to take home.

No one had explained who Wendy Hollender was, but as luck would have it, she happened to round the corner at the moment Beth was about to. Wendy could tell her story so casually, so candidly, almost as if she were talking about someone else. She might as well have been, because to these girls she looked and sounded so . . . so . . . normal.

Wendy knew otherwise, as did any survivor living with the memories and the fears that cancer would return. In casual locker room settings, even in Ireland with the teammates she trusted and loved, there were guarded moments when she was suddenly self-conscious about her body changes, her breast reconstruction. She wondered how they all would react.

Oh, what the hell, she decided as the Parlour Moms slipped out of their drenched clothes after they'd played their last game. It had been the kind of day, wild and wonderful, that draws adventure out from deep inside. "Does anyone want to see what a mastectomy and reconstruction looks like?" she blurted out.

Of course they did, and they marveled at Wendy's "new set." Soon the Parlour Moms in the nearby aisles were scurrying over and going topless, too, comparing and contrasting, complaining and celebrating. Wendy could step back then, no longer the center of attention, the "different" one. Soccer, as usual, was filling her life with normalcy, helping her cope. For a few glorious hours she could be the high school kid again. She could feel invulnerable, even if it was just until she got home and it was time to be the adult, to be Mom.

She deserved it, the chance to draw strength from them all, from these hysterical exchanges, this magical scene, from the ultimate team photo that no camera would record.

SHORT ON SUBSTITUTES, the Harps looked tired, water-logged, and beaten. Martha Kraeger, the former Holy Cross star, had already strafed them for four Xtreme goals from a variety of angles. Ravan had stoned them, throwing herself all over the slick turf, surrendering one goal when it might have been five.

Late in the game the Harps mustered one final burst of energy, a closing kick. They scored a second goal, then a third. Four–three, and still several minutes left. It took every bit of effort, a few fortunate bounces, all of the younger players on the field, and a couple of final theatrical saves by Ravan for the Xtreme to hold on. Time expired. Game and tournament over. It was half past four, after some seven hours spent in the rain, raising awareness and Cain.

Her hair all matted, Ravan charged from the net, clapping and yelping, "Way to go Xtreme–Badgers. We've got to keep this team together, do this again." Lisa hugged her teammates-for-the-time-being, and made plans with Minnie to mix the sides for the scheduled Xtreme–Badgers game at the dome the following Wednesday night. "That'll blow their minds at the dome," Lisa said.

Though her daughter's team and most of the Parlour Moms had gone, Wendy remained, with Maggie and Celia, to present the championship medals. As the players gathered round, Wendy, by now sheltered from the elements in a black winter jacket and red baseball cap, was summoned by Eileen Blair, the Montclair State coach, to take a bow and say a few words. Before she could say one, she was treated to a rousing round of applause.

Better yet, within several weeks Lisa, Venera, and Minnie Evans would pay tribute to Wendy in a more heartfelt and gratifying way: They formed their own nonprofit philanthropy group, calling it Goals for Life, and began planning their own charity tournament for June 2001.

Wendy, meanwhile, continued to solicit contributors for Teamwork. More donations rolled in. By midsummer, after all its bills for the symposium and tournament were paid, Teamwork 2000 had raised almost seven thousand dollars. Mount Sinai Hospital in Manhattan and St. Barnabas in Livingston had incorporated the fitness and well-being program Wendy had envisioned. She was already out walking the streets of Manhattan and the winding roads of Central Park with women undergoing treatment, helping put smiles on their faces. She had received Kevin McCarthy's commitment to use the Columbia University facilities for Teamwork 2001 the following spring.

Wendy felt as if she had scored her most meaningful goal. She would be eternally grateful to the Montclair women for their generous assist. "What I've always found amazing is how quickly you form meaningful relationships through soccer," she said.

The more Wendy learned about the Montclair women and about Lisa in particular, the more astonished she became at how much they had walked parallel paths. Long after she'd heard how Lisa had used soccer to alleviate her personal discomfort and stress, Wendy acknowledged her own private motivation for vigorously pursuing and playing this game—a secret she had kept through the most turbulent years of her life.

"Soccer was kind of a love affair, a way of having an exciting life, of filling a void," she said. Not long before she'd become ill, she had been close to ending her marriage, which she decided she had outgrown. Cancer put her plans and life on hold, but surviving the disease convinced her it was time to make the most of her precious life, time to conquer her fear of starting anew. She would within months make that leap she'd long ago planned.

As for Lisa, she could only marvel at the changes the sport had wrought. Nineteen months before, she had started with her list of twenty-four names, most of them of women she barely knew well enough to say hello to. Now, as thirty-two women posed for the Montclair group photo in front of the empty bleachers, Lisa drew satisfaction and strength from the realization that several of the pioneers—Venera and Dana, Rochelle and Jeanne, Barbara, the three Beths, and even a handful of Badgers—were still with her.

It would look like one extended happy family in the following week's *Montclair Times,* and even if that wasn't always the case, the big picture was the one to remember. The growing pains endured. The life's lessons learned.

Call it irony. Consider it fate. In the middle of the second row, Ravan Magrath was wedged between Rochelle Sandler, whose maternal advice she had once failed to heed, and Nina Sloan, whose ire she'd raised to the point of attack. One year after their scuffle in the dome, Ravan and Nina sat shoulder to shoulder, smile to smile. And nowhere in the photo or in the caption below was there even a suggestion of rain.

Epilogue

Playing for Keeps

WITH NO FORMAL INTRODUCTION, bound only by a wave and a Web site, Wendy Hollender and Jeanne Jeffrey drove off to New Hampshire on the July 4 weekend for their latest cross-river collaboration. They were on a reconnaissance mission to find the outer boundaries for a relatively inexperienced but dedicated soccer-playing mom. How far could they go? How good were the best? A new chapter, thought Wendy as she and Jeanne hit the open road.

Several weeks before the breast cancer event, Wendy had begun searching Web sites, calling around, and eventually hooked up with a most helpful source: Jan McFadden in Seattle. Wendy learned there were tournaments varying in levels of seriousness and quality that were fairly easy to enter. The daunting part, Jan warned her, was organizing the team, getting fifteen or more adult women away from their families and jobs. That in itself could almost become a full-time job.

The good news was that as women moved deeper and deeper into middle age and were less encumbered by young children at home, they could go greater distances, to more exotic locales. Out west there were women who played tournaments every weekend during spring and summer. They traveled to Hawaii, to Las Vegas, to a popular event called Soccer in the Sun in Puerto Vallarta.

Jan mentioned her and Bill's own vacation plans for early July, a trip to Nashua, New Hampshire, for the Veteran's Cup, which was considered by serious adult soccer players—male and female—the de facto national championship, under the auspices of the United States Amateur Soccer Association. There would be at least a couple of hundred women from around the country in the over-forties and over-fifties. Jan had played in 1998, in the first Veteran's Cup. The following year she served as team manager. At this point, nearing fory-nine, she knew she couldn't make the Copa de Vida team that would represent the state of Washington, but she would be fifty soon enough, and hoped to be playing in the nationals again before long.

Jan had been at this for twenty years now and knew the network. She told Wendy that some teams tended to be hodgepodge outfits mostly in it for the ride; with a little digging, Wendy might find a western squad short of players willing to make the cross-country trip.

Lisa would have joined Wendy in a heartbeat, but she was only thirty-eight: a comforting yet disappointing reality. Beth Fuqua, for once, wished her next birthday, her fortieth, had already passed. Everyone else seemed to have family plans, or was unprepared to make the plunge into so serious a competition. That left Jeanne Jeffrey, who was always ready to play, any game, anywhere. And Wendy by this time was in contact with a California Bay Area team, the Two Shays, who were, indeed, looking for players.

The Two Shays were a scattered lot from various Bay Area teams; Wendy and Jeanne, whose social history consisted of a quick greeting in the rain during the breast cancer tournament, fit right in. Over the next several weeks they familiarized themselves with one another on a team Web site, possibly making the Two Shays the world's first cyber sports team.

Back east, Wendy and Jeanne would log on to read the postings of their new "teammates"—Jan Archimede, Kim Northrup, Suzanne Lowe, Nancy Bovee. They were amazed at the intensity of their planning, the debating of every decision: the amount of practice they would need, the number of players, whether they had too many over-fifty players for a team that would be competing in an over-forty division.

They demanded honest appraisals of their respective abilities, of whether they could run at least five miles (the average distance running time in a soccer game) in eighty- to ninety-degree temperatures and in what might be oppressive humidity. Most admitted they couldn't. The answers reopened the debate on recruitment of more players, on positioning and playing time.

It was startling to Wendy and Jeanne how a day seldom passed without several of them posting their crowded soccer itineraries. "Like all they did was work and play soccer," Wendy said.

For some this was close to the truth, and they were proud to admit it. Connie Beal, a forty-eight-year-old real estate agent in Mountain View, called herself one of the "original soccer moms," though she acknowledged she was now known around the large Bay Area women's soccer community as an incorrigible "soccer slut."

Connie and her daughter, Christina, had been teammates for several years in the Bay Area Women's Soccer League, which had drawn so many players that it had split into seven divisions, ordered by skill. Soccer, she said, had given mother and daughter common ground through adolescence and her own marital breakup. Their team, the Storm, had by now moved up to the fifth division, where it was rolling along under the tutelage of Dimitri Kastis, who also happened to be the Two Shays' volunteer coach.

An engineer for Nokia in Mountain View, Dimitri was a forty-five-year-old bachelor who had played college soccer at Youngstown State in Ohio. He still played on various teams, coached a boys' select team and a coed team in addition to Connie's. He loved life, soccer, and women, he said, though not always in that particular order. "Playing soccer involves emotions, intelligence, team spirit, mind games, and more," Dimitri wrote in one Web posting. "I always thought that so much fun should not be the exclusive domain of men. Helping someone learn the sport I love is extremely rewarding."

Dimitri liberally shared his musings on the Two Shays' Web site. He posted his training expectations and practically sang his motivational mantras. He engaged in dialogues with the players, dispensing strategic and training advice with the self-assurance of a man on a mountain holding two tablets. He wrote Wendy a near treatise after she posed a question about making snap decisions on the attack once she was inside the scoring area: launch a blast off her strong left foot, or cross the ball with the hope of creating a better shot for someone else? All Dimitri was asking was that the women listen to him, that they play it his way. "Some say I am crazy to coach these women, who are soccer fanatics and have strong opinions, and none that I know, except Connie," he said.

As fate would have it, Dimitri would not know any of them: Connie Beal had been sent to the sidelines, hobbled by a clumsy male oaf. "I was playing lunchtime pickup, with men who were not experienced, which people have warned me not to do because they don't have the skills but they can't control their aggression," she wrote. "I was getting ready to kick one between the cones, and he threw his whole body into my left leg." She heard her knee pop. The orthopedist detected ligament damage. Surgery was a possibility, though one she wanted to avoid for fear of not being able to make it back. So New Hampshire was out, and Dimitri was on his own.

"Surrounded by sixteen strangers," he wrote, "bonding only with the unbreakable fiber of soccer."

On the Wednesday evening before the July 4 weekend, Wendy and Jeanne rendezvoused in Nashua with the Two Shays at the hotel bar and went about the task of putting faces to names, meeting all these women with whom they'd been sharing Web postings. Wendy, who had not shared her personal story on-line, discovered that a teammate was also a breast cancer survivor.

They all had soccer stories, a couple of decades' worth, including the most amazing one Wendy and Jeanne might ever hear. This went back to 1992 and, as Nancy Bovee told it, was about the woman who had more or less created the adult women's soccer movement in the Bay Area, during the mid- to late 1970s.

Lynn Barber had been a state junior hard-court tennis champion who took up soccer in middle age after watching and later refereeing her children's games. A psychiatric social worker, Lynn founded the Silicon Valley Soccer League, attracting many of the elite players in an area that produced the likes of Joy Fawcett and Brandi Chastain. She started an over-thirty division, just like the one in Seattle. From the older group she formed a select team to compete in tournaments. The San Andreas Fault, as it was called, went to Hawaii and shocked the mighty Blue Angels from Seattle on a Chastain-like penalty kick converted by Lynn.

Lynn's husband, Greg, a one-time college football assistant, coached the team, and in sixteen years he'd never missed one of her games—not until June 1992, when he put his assistant in charge for a tournament game at Stanford University and went off to do some chores.

By this time Lynn was a chain-smoker of long standing and had confided in her good friend Nancy that the results from a series of tests for cholesterol and blood pressure had come back dangerously high. Why Lynn would not tell her husband or visit Nancy's husband, a prominent Bay Area physician, Nancy never understood. Lynn was stubborn. She was naturally athletic, even while carrying too much weight.

None of the California women would ever forget the run to the goal Lynn made that terrible day, missing a shot and turning to jog back toward midfield—only to collapse, stricken with a heart attack and stroke, and die, at age fifty-five, before anyone could reach her.

Much later, after Nancy had planned Lynn's funeral because Greg was too grief-stricken, he told her of how Lynn had responded to the passing of an old friend in a cycling accident just a few days before her own untimely end. She was remarkably positive, saying again and again that at least he had died doing something he loved.

Greg had always loved coaching women because, as he said, "They are so damn good at bonding, and soccer's the game where everyone needs each other, and that is the secret to happiness, if you believe in relationships more than you do in material things." Of course, he had quit coaching in the years following Lynn's death, unable to so much as drive past the Stanford fields. But here was the incredibly uplifting part of the Lynn Barber story, as told by Nancy: Greg resumed coaching Lynn's friends in 1999. He had a girlfriend who was interested in the game, but he admitted that returning was about closure, about carrying on. It was a way to keep Lynn's spirit alive and honor the fact that she, too, had died doing something she loved.

After a long night of such storytelling, Wendy and Jeanne were ready to hit the practice field the following morning. They could barely wait. Almost immediately they realized that they could hold their own with the California women, who were obviously skilled but not the fittest players they'd ever seen. Eleven of the sixteen were over fifty, and one was over sixty. Wendy and Jeanne were used to playing against younger women, like the Harps in the Bronx Irish League and the Madness in Montclair. They felt good about themselves after the morning practice, and even better during an optional afternoon session, when most of the California women went off on a sightseeing trip.

They practically had Dimitri to themselves, which, Wendy said, was alone worth the drive. Dimitri Kastis was a trip—tan and handsome, about five-six, with more toned muscles than a man who ate so much ice cream had any right to have. On one excursion to a local ice cream store, he downed two scoops of chocolate and four milk shakes. He was just as hungry to teach the game: all business on the field, a natural teacher, positive and warm, willing and able to analyze all aspects of a game he'd literally had pounded into him from the time he was three.

"I remember my father sitting me on a table with pillows behind me," he said. "He would then throw at my head a soccer ball, and it would knock me backward onto the pillows. I would laugh my heart out and, needless to say, it left a big impression in my mind, not to mention some brain damage."

Wendy and Jeanne had never experienced this kind of personalized coaching. By that night, hours before they would play their first game against Copa de Vida, the defending champions from Washington State, they were practically giddy with anticipation. Jeanne went to sleep thinking, Piece of cake.

Then they hit the lobby the following morning and were startled by the sight of the other teams. Everyone, it seemed, was so tall, so slim, so . . . so . . . athletic! The women who were apparently over fifty didn't look a day over forty. The women who were supposed to be over forty didn't look a day over thirty.

"We may have to ask for birth certificates here," Jeanne said.

"No fat," said Wendy.

"No wrinkles," said Jeanne.

Epilogue

Minutes into their first game against the Washington women—led by Denise Bender, captain of the 1985 U.S. national team—it was crystal clear that the Two Shays had no chance. They couldn't keep up and were crushed, 8–0.

Wendy was "amazed, blown away, a little demoralized" by the speed and skill. The naturally fast Jeanne was able to keep pace, but skill-wise there wasn't all that much she could do except get physical. The old rugby player in her inevitably surfaced and earned her a few dirty looks for knocking over a couple of the Washington women with her team hopelessly behind. She would later say it had more to do with exhaustion. She wasn't used to playing ninety minutes, on full-size fields, or even on regular grass. "Indoors, in the dome, you just kick the ball on the ground and it goes where you want it to," she said. "Lifting the ball outside just to pass it ahead takes much more effort."

By the time the second game (a 4–0 defeat to a team from West Virginia) was over, Wendy realized the Two Shays were out of their league, and would have been better off entered in the B division, if not the over-fifties. She more or less resigned herself to receiving "a soccer education." Wendy initiated so many conversations with other players and coaches that her teammates dubbed her "the reporter." "These are the best over-forty and over-fifty women's players in the world, women who've been playing for twenty years," she said.

Even a hard-core veteran like Jan McFadden said she was stunned by what she saw, and she didn't mean the sights of New England. The adult women's game, her game, was growing right before her eyes into something widespread and wonderful. In 1998 the first Veteran's Cup she had played in was a modest gathering, nine teams, men and women. Now there were thirty-nine teams from nineteen states. Sixty-four, half of them women, were expected for the 2001 tournament in West Virginia. "It's a joy to watch," she said. "There's much more talent than in the last two years."

The Two Shays, eliminated from contention by Friday afternoon, had one last game on Saturday, against a team from New Hampshire. By this time Nancy Bovee had limped off to the sideline to join a couple of others. They were down to twelve or thirteen healthy players. Jeanne was moved up to forward to take advantage of her speed. She and Wendy, playing a variety of positions, were told by Dimitri that they would likely have to play the entire game.

The New Hampshire women were more on their level: less experienced but fit. Wendy got off a few hard left-footed shots. Jeanne broke through on a couple of her patented runs and almost scored. It was a warm day, and Jeanne played all out, every minute. When the game ended, 0–0, she was flat on her back, sucking air, never this tired in her life. Her new California friends, appreciating the effort, dumped water all over her. Dimitri said he was proud of her. They took team photos and video. The Two Shays, finishing the tournament without a goal to their name, still managed to go their separate sightseeing ways feeling accomplished and proud.

Jeanne went off to Cape Cod to spend the rest of the weekend. Wendy drove down to Boston to visit her brother and his family. She thought she'd had enough soccer for the weekend, but she awoke on Sunday and couldn't help herself: She talked her nine-year-old niece into making the drive back to Nashua with her for the championship game.

Copa from Washington would be defending its over-forty women's title against the Camp Spring Soccer Club from Maryland. And there on the sideline were Jan McFadden with her granddaughter and Wendy with her niece, two women in their forties, two role models who loved the game and who had in common the conviction that playing this sport had given them strength and guided them through their darkest days.

Nothing against Jan, but Wendy had to admit that she was rooting her heart out for the Maryland team. The Washington women were the Boston Celtics and New York Yankees of adult women's soccer: Pulling for the underdog, for the team that had to catch up, just seemed natural for a woman who had not even kicked a ball until she was forty. Time makes its run at everyone, though. Competition is a growth product. The Maryland women scored a goal in the twentieth minute, and held on for a tense and fiercely fought 1–0 win.

Wendy went home happy and energized. She and Jeanne continued their on-line relationships with the Two Shays, especially after Wendy weeks later tore the anterior cruciate ligament in her right knee ("my non-shooting leg, thank God," she said) and needed medical advice from Connie Beal, among others, who welcomed her to "knee-brace hood." Some years earlier, Wendy had watched her husband, a longtime runner, become inactive and practically immobilized by a less severe knee injury. After all she'd been through, this was not going to happen to her. She vowed to be back on the field for Lisa's Montclair tournament in June, if not for Teamwork 2001, in April.

The fiber of soccer, meanwhile, was also growing stronger between Manhattan and Montclair. Wendy invited Jeanne to be an honorary Parlour Mom for their three-day getaway to Shelter Island in August. New Hampshire, Wendy and Jeanne agreed, had been one fantastic adventure, and if they brought home any particular message, it was that they all had much to look forward to, many experiences ahead.

At forty-five they already knew there was a limit to what they could expect of themselves, if only for another few years. "Five more years' experience," Wendy said, "and hopefully when I reach the over-fifties I will catch up to those women."

Jeanne, for her part, said: "I never thought I'd ever look forward to the day I actually turned fifty."

Epilogue

Now it was time to spread the word at home about the big, bad, and beautiful world.

A S 2001 APPROACHED, Lisa and friends were preparing to have the women's soccer world come to them. Combining their professional skills to launch Goals for Life, they were planning a forty-team tournament with multiple skill divisions for the following June. Lisa, Venera, and Minnie had recruited, among other volunteers, Bobbi Brown as a cochairwoman. They were targeting all proceeds for their maiden event to the Susan G. Komen Breast Cancer Foundation. "Keep life in perspective, have a purpose each day," Lisa wrote as part of her promotional pitch.

The Montclair women's soccer movement was now two years old, and she didn't have to sell the game to mothers anymore. Thanks in large part to her, it was an accepted fixture in town. The women were a presence, rushing either through business districts in their team jerseys or Teamwork T-shirts, or into the Soccer Domain, where adult women players claimed the field no fewer than four nights a week. Ashley's trainers had moved the Soccer Moms programs into neighboring towns and it also wasn't long before there were weekday morning outdoor games on full-sized fields, eleven versus eleven, home-and-home series, mimicking the kids' travel teams.

The women were athletic activists, role models to their children and other people's children. Several became licensed youth coaches and league commissioners and informed sources of soccer information. They were students of the game. Yet they delivered their most powerful message, made their most potent points, just by lacing up their cleats with the attitude that it wasn't an issue anymore; soccer was part of their weekly curriculum and family schedule. The game was no Beanie Babies or Pokémon fad that would inevitably fade. Their husbands realized this, as did their children, now remarkably conditioned to the fair and uncontestable notion that when Mom was playing, you stayed out of the way. You let her be.

In Brookdale Park, egos were reined in. Perspective reigned. Here, where it had all begun with one kick of the ball, the soccer moms were at their best. Rick Telander's landmark book on pickup basketball years ago contended that heaven is a playground, but the park too could be paradise on a crisp summer evening when a couple of dozen mothers would take the field and their children would run off in the distance to organize themselves. When strollers and joggers would stop and watch and inevitably go off with sappy smiles. When every few minutes another car would ease around the bend and roll to the curb, and one more player for the weekly pickup game would rush down the grassy incline, lugging water bottle and ball, no longer just a children's ritual. This was, in fact, the very spot where the kids were dropped off for soccer camp, and the teenage counselors would pull open the car doors and Ashley Hammond would greet them as they scampered by to locate their group.

One late-summer night, Ashley sat cross-legged in the grass to the rear left of a netless goal, furiously taking notes on a white sheet of paper.

"I'm charting Meg," he said, his eyes fixed on the field, on his wife. "She says that I never watch her play. So this will prove to her I do."

Ashley had to admit that, these days, the females commanding his most rapt attention were a group of ten-year-old girls. He was conducting his own little gender equity experiment, proving— mostly to himself—that girls would respond to the rigorous year-round training demands traditionally made on boys. The Aristocats, as they were called, were playing older girls, in the highest division, or flight. Meg's daughter, Annie, was the family Aristocat, but even Mom had an ego, a need for "Coach" to take notice.

"Back pass . . . bad cross . . . sideline tackle." Mouthing the notations as he scribbled them in pencil, Ashley chuckled, amused by the thought of his wife reading through them later.

His little family joke was in no way meant to poke fun at the soccer moms. He continued to be amazed by their improving play and was now seeing the same process at work at clinics his staff were running in neighboring towns. All things considered, after all the dabbling and squabbling, all the Badger bashing, having had these women move off the sideline had been the best thing to happen to Ashley's organization—and by extension, to the children who were tethered to it—in years.

He agreed that Lisa had been a singular driving force (though she was the first to say that Ashley and his staff had played a substantial role in the formation of the women's soccer community). But given the contentious demand for field time in the dome, Ashley could easily have filled it without the women and saved himself considerable grief in the process. He was admittedly frustrated at times, accused of profiteering, for just being the Man in what was essentially a women's venture. Ashley maintained the women's leagues were more than a good business opportunity: They were a source of professional pride. It was his unabashed opinion that they had all helped foster something of a new social order in town, serving in some respects as a twenty-first-century version of the community church group.

Beyond their emerging philanthropic bent, the mothers were innovative and inclusive, doing sports much differently than men. The anniversary party at the dome was one example. A Pokémoms' dinner and holiday party at Cathy Wright's house was another. When Beth Fuqua rented the dome for her fortieth-birthday soccer bash, an old friend toasted her for celebrating "the next forty years as opposed to reliving the last forty."

"The men only want to come in, beat the hell out of each other for an hour, maybe go out for a beer, and go home," Ashley said. "The women are different, smarter. They demand more out of it, and they get more out of it."

They were still enduring their own trials and tribulations at the dome, week to week, season to season. But nothing like the men, whose leagues were marred by aggression that bordered on violence and had become so vexing that Bob Stanton, who managed the leagues, instituted a dome-wide ban on slide tackling with Ashley's blessing. It was only an experiment, a summer trial, but when the word got out, Beth Fuqua couldn't help but feel vindicated for the antislide-tackle stand she had taken more than a year before. The model could, apparently, be reinvented after all.

Here in the park the pickup games weren't quite scoreless basketball, but they were freewheeling, fun-loving, uplifting. It was no coincidence that many of the women said they preferred them to the actual league games, much the way wishful baby boomers lament the overly competitive structure of their children's recreational lives. Of course, there was ideology and there was reality. Many of these same parents sometimes acted as if it was never too early for their kids to begin grinding away at sports in the hope of earning a scholarship, however infinitesimal their chances might be.

Never had there been a generation of children more driven under watchful adult eyes to strive and succeed on the athletic fields. Psychologists had been warning for years that youth sports were becoming too important, too scripted, and that something as heated and physical as competitive athletics could combine with parental partisanship to form an explosive compound. Sure enough, a sobering case out of Reading, Massachusetts, where one hockey father beat another to death, thrusting the issue of parental sports rage into the national spotlight in July 2000. No less a source than *Sports Illustrated* presented the compelling case against "a new species of bird" it called "Parentis vociferous" in a special report entitled "Out of Control."

"Loud, intrusive moms and dads [who are] unable to restrain themselves," the magazine called these parents. And while it would be foolish and naïve to suggest that mothers everywhere were having no trouble controlling their sideline emotions, *Sports Illustrated* did not comment upon the clear pattern of its own reporting: Of the violent and disheartening incidents the story chronicled, all but one involved men.

Perhaps having women play a greater role, an equal role, in steering the athletic lives of their children wasn't a solution in itself. But few could deny that it was getting a little crazy out there, and that baby boomer fathers who'd grown up fancying themselves athletes were more likely to live vicariously through their children. It couldn't hurt to have Mom's nurturing presence counter Dad's need to succeed.

Women didn't have all the answers, but as the Montclair soccer-playing mothers demonstrated over and over, they were more likely at least to stop to consider the questions. Through their own experiences they came to the understanding that participating in a recreational team sport was not about putting on blinders and running all out. It was more a marathon than a hundred-meter dash, requiring careful planning, pacing, and a perspective that demanded periodical adjustments in operation and expectation.

The Pokémoms became a prime example of this, as their opposition took on younger players and their proposal for an over-thirty league remained unrealized. By the middle of summer 2000, they were tired of being the intermediate league doormat. They were tired, even, of being Pokémoms; their kids were no longer trading the cards, the concept was no longer cute, and the truth was that they no longer wanted to be thought of as cute.

Epilogue

They understood that they were in a league that had no angel of equality, no Cindy Aserkoff, to choose up equal sides, to legislate the score out. The Pokémoms had tried their own experiment, one quite different from Ashley's. Socially, it was wonderful; athletically, it was . . . educational. It was time to move on, though. Time to retire Cathy Wright's Pokémom shirts, as Lisa had those of the Bluestone Belles.

Nina Sloan had had enough of being a human target in a shooting gallery. Beth Fuqua was drained by the feelings of responsibility for having organized the group. Along the string of demoralizing defeats, they all went home, week after week, feeling pangs of guilt for the complaints they found themselves whispering to one another about which player was too indifferent, too negative, and, yes, too much of a liability. So they surrendered, finally and wholeheartedly, to the inevitability of wanting to win, while maintaining they would never allow themselves to become defined by or obsessed with winning.

They devised, not without great pains and a few bruised egos, a plan to divide the roster, to seek out new players to make each side better equipped to compete with the ever-changing league. Teetering on the fringes of the Xtreme lineup, Clare Moore, Dana DiMuro, and the young Irishwoman, Mary Burke, dropped down to the intermediate league, rejoining Barbara Martoglio, Ellen Paretti, and Beth Albert in a virtual Bluestone Belles reunion. Meg Hammond, meanwhile, resumed playing with the Pokémoms' other half, and one glorious night, days after Mary Burke was sworn in as a U.S. citizen in Newark, she scored a goal and the dome erupted in cheers of "U.S.A. . . . U.S.A."

"The one thing I think was hardest for people to accept was that soccer was always going to be changing, that it had to be fluid," Lisa said. "For a long time I don't know if everyone fully understood that."

Lisa's own team was down to Venera, Jeanne, and herself from the original Belles. But she understood, better than most, that every sports team in every season is an experiment in social dynamics, among other things. Experience taught you to roll with failure, to shrug and move on. After agonizing so much about the start-up almost two years before, after all the fussing and feuding and, most significantly, all the personal changes she had made, how could Lisa, of all people, not view her involvement in broader, conceptual terms?

"When I see a skilled player out there now, I find myself wanting to applaud, whether the person is on my team or another team, whether that person is young or old," she said. "On game nights now, I'll often stay for both games, just because I enjoy being around, and it makes me feel good to watch someone else do well. I'm always amazed at what some of these women can do."

She might have been talking about herself, or Wendy Hollender in New York, or those out west. Women who had had ideas and the determination to execute them and had watched them grow into something big and bold.

It was impossible to calculate how many adult women were playing competitive soccer, or even just kicking a ball around a symmetrical arrangement of cones. In the aftermath of the Women's World Cup and the 2000 Olympics in Sydney, estimates by various soccer organizations ranged from a couple hundred thousand to more than a half million. Whatever the actual tally, it was by all accounts growing. Stories continued to appear in major newspapers across the country about women who were crossing the line, taking the field. Once across, once in control of their bodies and the ball, most would find there was no turning back.

"As long as my back doesn't give way, I'll keep working hard and play on whatever teams I can," Lisa said one day, waiting for two of her children to finish a session of Ashley's Soccer Camp, a ball at her foot and her oldest daughter, Olivia, beckoning her to pass. "I want to go with it as far as I can." Two years after her first strike she was going back to the sideline, temporarily. Lisa and Kevin McGrath, the soccer trainer who was now her significant other, were expecting her fourth child.

Months before, she had considered a hypothetical question about the difficult sacrifices female athletes of every generation have had to make, and will surely be making in greater numbers in the coming years. "As a woman, the choice to have a child would not be difficult," she'd said. "As an athlete, I would try to stay involved in the watching, the coaching, and after the baby was born, I would use the game as a way to motivate myself to get back in shape. I would want to balance both."

Not surprisingly, Lisa's pregnancy set off another brief round of did-ya-hear in town, which she expected, and ignored. It was her baby, her business, and her belief that while her children and family matters were surely no game, there was an important lesson to be learned from soccer, an inspirational metaphor at midfield. There would always be change to deal with and obstacles on the way to the goal, but there was only one way to get there: keep moving forward, keep kicking, on a parallel course with life.

Acknowledgments

THIS PROJECT BEGAN with a nine-hundred-word newspaper story, the uncertain notion that there might be a way of developing it, and a providential telephone call to a soccer mom in suburban Chicago, my incredibly supportive agent, Shari Wenk. Without her guidance and determination, this book would not exist. Likewise my editor at Simon & Schuster, Jeff Neuman, whose wisdom focused and tightened the story and made it so much easier to tell. I am forever grateful to both.

One of the least attractive aspects of covering professional sports is the inevitable reality that many athletes will do whatever they can to avoid you. For more than a year I had the opportunity and privilege of imposing myself on the wonderfully cluttered lives of so many "real" people, and was not once told to take a hike or to contact an agent. I truly appreciate all that time, and the chance to have learned so much.

Regrettably, some of the athletes whose accommodation guided me as the project took shape early on did not become featured players. Lisa Springer and Cristina Delgado, and the Brooklyn Blades hockey team should especially understand that their stories were as inspirational and instrumental in creating the book as any I heard. Cindy Aserkoff was delightfully insistent on helping me redefine the meaning of *athlete*. I would also like to thank Professor Mary Jo Kane for shedding light on this most worthwhile subject and directing me as my feet moved forward.

Fortunately, those early steps led me to Seattle, and to Jan and Bill McFadden, who opened my eyes to the possibilities for adult women's soccer—in addition to the breathtaking lake view from their living room. Jan, in turn, kindly introduced me to, among others, Bernadette Noonan and Janet Slauson, and what an education that turned out to be.

Of course, the core of the story developed—literally at times—right in my own backyard. To every single one of the women of the Montclair leagues, a heartfelt thank-you for sharing so much in countless interviews and casual chats. To Lisa Ciardi, for trying to put aside her modest inclination not to make this about herself. To Beth Fuqua, for being such a fair and accurate "reporter." To my Beth (Albert), for being able to tolerate (most of the time) her husband lurking nearby.

I am grateful to Ashley and Meg Hammond for their personal and professional cooperation. Also to the many members of their staff, including Bob Stanton and, in particular, Vanessa Hardwick. And, as the boundaries of the story widened, how lucky I was to make the acquaintance of Wendy Hollender, whose energy and faith inspire everyone she meets.

For their encouragement and assistance, I would be remiss in not mentioning Howard Kerbel, Ellen Paretti, Brian Ciardi, Ed and Barbara Martoglio, Ian and Cathy Wright, Susan and Arthur Hatzopoulos, and Beth and Tom Panucci. I was also fortunate to have had the invaluable friendship and professional wisdom of Michelle Musler, Ed Lopez, Ernestine Miller, Robert Cumins, Dominick Anfuso, Bob Drury, Pam and Richard Satran, Marty and Kathy Beiser, Selena Roberts, Gwen Knapp, Johnette Howard, Lisa Dillman, Ailene Voisin, Lena Williams, Barry Stanton, Howard Blatt, Filip Bondy, Neil Amdur, Mike Wise, Jay Schreiber, and Bill Brink.

Finally, I would like to thank the other soccer players in the family. Alex and Charlie, I am so proud of you for being so proud of your mother.

About the Author

HARVEY ARATON is a sports columnist for *The New York Times* who was nominated for the Pulitzer Prize in 1994 and was honored for column writing by the Women's Sports Foundation in 1998. He previously co-authored *The Selling of the Green* and *Money Players*, both about pro basketball. He lives in Montclair, New Jersey.